CAMBRIDGE LIBRARY COLLECTION

Books of enduring scholarly value

Polar Exploration

This series includes accounts, by eye-witnesses and contemporaries, of early expeditions to the Arctic and the Antarctic. Huge resources were invested in such endeavours, particularly the search for the North-West Passage, which, if successful, promised enormous strategic and commercial rewards. Cartographers and scientists travelled with many of the expeditions, and their work made important contributions to earth sciences, climatology, botany and zoology. They also brought back anthropological information about the indigenous peoples of the Arctic region and the southern fringes of the American continent. The series further includes dramatic and poignant accounts of the harsh realities of working in extreme conditions and utter isolation in bygone centuries.

A Voyage to Hudson's Bay during the Summer of 1812

Thomas M'Keevor served as the physician for the second group of Selkirk settlers that set out in 1812 for the Red River Colony in Canada. This short account of what he witnessed, particularly the crossing of Hudson Bay, appeared in 1819. Greatly interested in icebergs, M'Keevor discusses these 'sea mountains' in detail. He also describes the Inuit peoples encountered, giving a short glossary of Inuit words. Presenting a vivid account of the scene, he was clearly moved by seeing a polar bear protecting her cubs from a hunting party sent out from the ship. Also published in this volume is a brief account in English of the 1806 voyage of the *Sirène* by the French naval officer Fréminville. Initially tasked with attacking British whalers off Spitsbergen, the frigate came close to the coast of Greenland, yet most of the time on land was spent in Iceland, where observations were made of the Icelandic people, fauna and geology.

Cambridge University Press has long been a pioneer in the reissuing of out-of-print titles from its own backlist, producing digital reprints of books that are still sought after by scholars and students but could not be reprinted economically using traditional technology. The Cambridge Library Collection extends this activity to a wider range of books which are still of importance to researchers and professionals, either for the source material they contain, or as landmarks in the history of their academic discipline.

Drawing from the world-renowned collections in the Cambridge University Library and other partner libraries, and guided by the advice of experts in each subject area, Cambridge University Press is using state-of-the-art scanning machines in its own Printing House to capture the content of each book selected for inclusion. The files are processed to give a consistently clear, crisp image, and the books finished to the high quality standard for which the Press is recognised around the world. The latest print-on-demand technology ensures that the books will remain available indefinitely, and that orders for single or multiple copies can quickly be supplied.

The Cambridge Library Collection brings back to life books of enduring scholarly value (including out-of-copyright works originally issued by other publishers) across a wide range of disciplines in the humanities and social sciences and in science and technology.

A Voyage to Hudson's Bay
during the Summer of 1812

*Containing a Particular Account
of the Icebergs and Other Phenomena
which Present Themselves in those Regions;
Also, a Description of the Esquimeaux
and North American Indians*

THOMAS M'KEEVOR

CAMBRIDGE
UNIVERSITY PRESS

CAMBRIDGE
UNIVERSITY PRESS

University Printing House, Cambridge, CB2 8BS, United Kingdom

Published in the United States of America by Cambridge University Press, New York

Cambridge University Press is part of the University of Cambridge.

It furthers the University's mission by disseminating knowledge in the pursuit of education, learning and research at the highest international levels of excellence.

www.cambridge.org
Information on this title: www.cambridge.org/9781108071505

© in this compilation Cambridge University Press 2014

This edition first published 1819
This digitally printed version 2014

ISBN 978-1-108-07150-5 Paperback

ISLAND OF RESOLUTION AT THE ENTRANCE TO HUDSONS STRAITS.

N.º VIII.

A

VOYAGE

TO

HUDSON'S BAY,

DURING THE SUMMER

OF 1812.

CONTAINING

A PARTICULAR ACCOUNT OF THE ICEBERGS AND OTHER
PHENOMENA WHICH PRESENT THEMSELVES
IN THOSE REGIONS;

ALSO,

A DESCRIPTION OF THE ESQUIMEAUX AND NORTH AME-
RICAN INDIANS; THEIR MANNERS, CUSTOMS,
DRESS, LANGUAGE, &c. &c. &c.

BY

THOMAS M'KEEVOR, M.D.

OF THE DUBLIN LYING-IN HOSPITAL.

Where, undissolving from the first of time,
Snows swell on snows amazing to the sky,
And icy mountains, high on mountains pil'd,
Seem, to the shivering sailor, from afar,
Shapeless and white, an atmosphere of clouds
Projecting, huge and horrid, o'er the surge.

LONDON:

PRINTED FOR SIR RICHARD PHILLIPS AND Co.
BRIDE-COURT, BRIDGE-STREET.

1819.

W. Lewis, Printer, 21, Finch-lane, Cornhill.

PREFACE.

A few months relaxation from professional studies during the summer of the year 1812, and a very liberal offer of the Earl of Selkirk, induced me to become the medical attendant on his Lordship's colony, then about to depart for Hudson's Bay.

The notes which I took during that very interesting voyage, have lain by me ever since; nor is it probable they would ever have emerged from obscurity, but for the unprecedented interest which the affairs of that part of the northern world have of late excited, and for the present convenient and popular form of publication.

The literary defects which pervade this narrative require, I am aware, some apology; but this, I should hope, will be afforded by the unremitting anxieties to which I am exposed in my present situation of Assistant to the extensive Lying-in Hospital of this city.

Dublin Lying-in Hospital,
Aug. 26, 1819.

VOYAGE

TO

HUDSON'S BAY.

O N Wednesday, June the 24th, about four o'clock in the afternoon, we got under way, having on-board the Earl of SELKIRK, Mr. EVERARD of Sligo, and a few other gentlemen who had dined with us. At first it was our intention not to proceed to sea that night, but merely to get clear of Sligo Bay, which cannot at all times be easily accomplished. About six o'clock, however, the captain came down to inform Lord Selkirk, that it was his wish to proceed to sea immediately; and Lord Selkirk and company took their leave.

Their "lessening boat" had scarcely disappeared, when, leaning over the quarter-deck, I was insensibly led to the contemplation of the grand and sublime scenery with which I was, for the first time in my life, surrounded. On one side I beheld the vast and widely-extended body of waters, over which the moon was just beginning to throw a diffused and silvery light; on the other appeared my native land, like a dusky streak stretched along the verge of the horizon. Its thin and misty form had somewhat the appearance of a dense vapour, which had been precipitated by the chill cool air of evening.

The solemnity and stillness of this calm repose of nature was only interrupted by the soft splash of the light wave against the head and sides of the vessel, and occasionally by the slow and solemn voice of the captain giving his commands to the helmsman.

From this train of reflections I was, however, soon disturbed by the voice of the steward, who came upon deck to announce that supper was on the table. I immediately went down to the cabin, where I found Mr. and Mrs. M'Clain, from the Isle of Mull; Mr. Keveny, Mr. Johnson, and the rest of the cabin-passengers. After partaking of a very elegant and well-dressed supper, we continued chatting until twelve o'clock: "that hour o' night's black arch the keystone," when we all agreed to retire, or, as it is technically termed, to *turn in.* In a short time, without much solicitation, we were visited by that sweet refreshing power which rarely visits sorrow, and when it doth, it is a comforter.

During the first week, the occurrences of our voyage were

like the generality of sea-affairs, too trivial to become interesting, and too unvaried to afford amusement. The wind continued fair, and the weather extremely fine, so that on an
average we made about 150 miles each day.

Thursday, July the 2d. Early in the morning, we observed
a strange sail, which the captain at first apprehended might
be an enemy; but, on nearer approach, he discovered her to
be the King George, one of the Hudson's Bay company's ships,
commanded by Captain Turner: a short time after, we observed another vessel, which we found to be the Eddystone,
the property of the same company, commanded by Captain
Ramsay. At nine o'clock, A. M. they continued to bear down
upon us in full sail. About ten we spoke the King George;
and, shortly after, the Eddystone, lat. as observed, 57° 43′ N.;
we continued in company for a couple of hours. Our vessel,
however, being much better adapted for quick sailing, we, in
a short time, left them completely behind.

Sunday, July the 12th. Weather very thick and hazy, accompanied with constant drizzling rain. Wind continues fair.
The air feels very cold, owing, as the captain suspects,
to our being near ice. About half past one, the man at the
helm said he saw land. Owing to the very unfavourable
state of the weather, we remained for a considerable time in
suspense. The captain does not think that this can possibly
be the case. At length, however, from its very striking appearance, he was induced to send for his telescope; is still
rather doubtful; if land, he thinks, it must be Cape Farewell,*
in which case we are 200 miles behind where we supposed ourselves to be. In the end, it appeared to be merely what the
seamen call a *Cape Fly-away.*

About two o'clock the captain, having got an interval of
fine weather, set about making an observation, which satisfied him that we were then past the entrance to Davis's
Straits. About four o'clock we saw a young whale.

Monday, July the 13th. The weather continues thick and
hazy, with much rain, but little wind; helm lashed. Air
still feels very cold, especially on going aloft.

About nine o'clock, P. M., two men were stationed at the
bow of the vessel, that immediate notice might be given of the
appearance of ice. The captain, before going to bed, gave
orders that ice-anchors, boat-hooks, &c. should be got in readiness. Twelve o'clock, P. M., wind increased, going about

---

* Cape Farewell, the southern extremity of Greenland, is situated in
lat. 59° 38′ N., and long. 42° W.

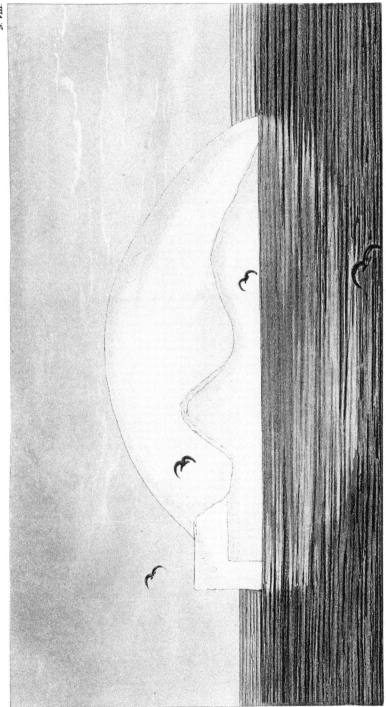

AN ISLAND OF ICE.

three knots; took in sail. About one we lay to. About half-past one, P. M., we saw ice for the first time; it appeared* in the form of large detached masses. Several pieces struck the vessel, and with so much violence as to awaken almost every person on board. Four o'clock : the ice continues to come in immense large fleaks ; the pieces are larger, but not quite so numerous. Owing to the very unfavourable state of the weather, we could get no opportunity for making an observation ; the captain, however, suspects that we are about the entrance to Hudson's Straits.

Tuesday, July the 14th. Weather still continues thick and hazy; almost a complete calm; helm lashed. The horizon is covered with numerous fleaks of ice ; on some of them we observed a great quantity of sand and gravel. Some of these masses had a greenish, while others had an azure tint; they appeared to be moving with considerable velocity.

About five o'clock in the afternoon we saw the first island of ice ; the haze of the atmosphere, along with a light drizzling rain, prevented us, however, from seeing either its summit or circumference distinctly. Plate II. will afford a tolerable correct idea of its appearance; it was taken by Mr. Holmes, an ingenious young gentleman, who was *on his way out* to join Lord Selkirk's party on Red River. This enormous mass appeared quite stationary; at least, I could not observe that it had the slightest motion.

Friday, July the 17th. About six o'clock in the morning the captain came down to inform us that he had seen land ; is uncertain, however, where we are, not having had any opportunity of making an observation for some days. Is inclined to think, *however,* that it is Resolution-Island.†

About nine o'clock we got within a short distance of it; it had a most cheerless, dreary appearance, being for the most

---

* In clear weather a curious appearance, to which seamen have given the name of the Ice-blink, is observed on approaching the ices. It consists of a lucid streak spread along that part of the atmosphere which is next the horizon. It is evidently occasioned by the reflection of the rays of light which fall on the surface of the ice into the superincumbent air. Not unfrequently they afford a beautiful map or picture of the ice for a considerable distance, resembling, in this way, the curious atmospherical phenomenon to which naturalists have given the name of the Mirage. Field-ice, Mr. Scoresby informs us, affords the most lucid blink, accompanied with a tinge of yellow: that of *packs* is more peculiarly white, and of *bay-ice* greyish. The land, from its snowy covering, likewise occasions a blink, which is yellowish, and not unlike that produced by the ice of fields.

† Resolution Island is situated on the N. side of the entrance into Hudson's Straits; it is considered to be about sixty miles in circumference, N. lat. 61° 40′ W. long. 65°.

part covered with frost and snow, with, here and there, patches of dark black peat. Not a single shrub enlivened this barren desolate spot. Here every thing wore a solitary, sad, and dismal aspect. The hoarse murmuring of the waves, which ever and anon renewed their assaults on the huge masses of dark-grey rock that opposed them, gave it, I thought, a still more despondent look.

Ten o'clock. After bearing away from the land, we again got in among straggling ice.

After dinner, this day, Mr. Johnson came down to the cabin in great agitation to inform us that we were bearing fast down on an immense mountain of ice.* A solemn pause ensued on hearing this very alarming piece of intelligence. In a short time, however, we were all upon deck; and here the appearance of our situation was awful in the extreme; the shouting of the men, the rumbling of the cordage, the tremendous mountain of ice, on which we every moment expected to be dashed to pieces, contributed to render this scene the most terrific that could well be imagined. The captain did all he could to get the ship about, but without effect, owing to her having missed stays. We were not more than ten yards from it, when fortunately a light breeze springing up, the sails filled, and in a short time we were completely clear of this frightful mass. Plate III. affords a very correct representation of it.

The whole of this day was truly unpleasant; the weather continued thick and hazy; indeed, the fog was at times so dense that we could hardly see ten yards from the ship, in consequence of which we were frequently just in contact with fields of ice without being at all aware of it. Friday night

---

* The British Packet, Lady Hobart, ran against one of these floating islands, higher than the mast-head, and of great extent, in June, 1803, and foundered; the crew and passengers saved themselves with great difficulty in two boats. The American ship Neptune perished likewise in the same manner, with a great part of the people in her. Captain Cotes, of the Hudson's-Bay Company's service, lost two ships in a similar way; one of them by running against a piece of ice in the night, off Cape Farewell, in consequence of which the ship foundered; the other in Hudson's Straits, where two large fields of ice were driven together with great force; the ship being between them, was so much damaged that she sunk as soon as the ice departed. Mr. Ellis tells us, that one of the Hudson's-Bay Company's ships was caught in a similar way, while on her way from York-Fort to Churchill; upon the two pieces meeting, she was raised quite out of the water, and left dry upon one of them; but she receiving no damage by that strange accident, when the ice opened, the people launched her, and proceeded on their voyage.—*See Ellis's Voyage to Hudson's Bay,* p. 67.

THE FIELD OF ICE AGAINST WHICH THE SHIP WAS STRIKING.

it continued to blow very fresh ; constantly tacking between land and ice. Ship got several very severe knocks; so severe, indeed, thát a considerable quantity of copper has been torn from her bottom.

Saturday, July the 18th. Weather continues squally, with dense fog. Still tacking about between land and ice. Uncertain of our situation, the captain not being able to make any observation. Also uncertain of our course, in consequence of the extraordinary variation of the compass.* The ship became so leaky this day, in consequence of the injuries received from the ice, that we were obliged to keep the pumps constantly at work.

Sunday, July 19th. Weather much improved; occasional sun-shine. About twelve, the captain was enabled to make an observation; found that we were in latitude 61° 26'. We were now quite satisfied that the land in view was Resolution-Island.

Four o'clock. Haze and mist completely dispersed: steady sun-shine. Wind much more moderate; patches of fine blue sky here and there present themselves. It is inconceivable with what joy we beheld the first gleam of sun-shine; its cheering beams appeared to diffuse cheerfulness and good-humour amongst us all. About six, we were completely surrounded with ice; the wind, however, became so moderate, that we ran no risk by venturing in amongst it. Several icebergs in view. Just as we had done dinner this day, the steward came into the cabin with word that the King George and Eddystone, the two vessels already mentioned, were in sight. Nothing could possibly have afforded us greater gratification than this intelligence. We all immediately went upon deck, when, to our very great surprise, we saw the George about thirty yards from us. The Eddystone, owing to the ice, could not get quite so near. In a short time, the George got so close that we were able to get on board by

---

* The exact cause of this extraordinary variation is, I believe, not well ascertained. The most generally received opinion, however, is, that which attributes it to the influence of some enormous mass of metallic matter contained in the bowels of the earth. By the early navigators, this phenomenon was ascribed to the cold air situated between the needle and the point of its attraction. Ellis asserts, that when the compasses were brought into a warm room, they recovered their proper action and direction; *i. e.* when brought down to the cabin it pointed with much greater accuracy. I may remark, that we found the same effect produced by bringing the boxes down to the cabin. Perhaps, in this case, the cold acted by congealing the moisture contained in the air which surrounded the needle, and in this way presented a mechanical obstruction to its motion.—The subject is curious.

merely crossing a single flake of ice. Here we spent a very
pleasant evening. After taking tea and other refreshments,
a dance was proposed. The Scotch piper was instantly sum-
moned upon deck, and I was much amused at the haughty
air with which this rawboned athletic highlander strutted up
and down, his plaiden pendant streaming in the air, while
the pitroch sent forth its shrill-inspiring peal through the
adjacent hills and vallies. After some preparatory arrange-
ments, the whole party, consisting of about eight couple,
were in brisk and rapid motion.

When the dance was ended, our musician, after some
introductory screams and flourishes, commenced the famous
battle song. For my part, I could discover nothing in this
favourite production of the Celtic muse, but a confused collection of harsh and dissonant sounds. On the faces of our
Caledonian friends, however, it appeared to operate like
magic : their hard and rigid features began to relax, the eye
began to sparkle, and the whole visage to assume a gay and
animated appearance, mixed, I thought, with some little portion of lofty unbending pride, which shewed itself particularly by a complacent smile that played about the angle of the
mouth. About twelve o'clock we sat down to a very elegant
supper, and soon forgot the perilous, I might say, the awful
situation, in which we were placed. We resolved on strewing
with flowers " the moments as they rolled," and gave ourselves
up for some hours to gaiety and mirth.

> The storm without might rain and rustle,
> Tam did na mind the storm a whistle.

About two o'clock we parted ; the moon had just emerged
from amidst a mass of dark black clouds, and poured her full
tide of effulgence on the surrounding scenery, giving it an
appearance, to borrow the words of a favourite, though unknown author, as if a covering of the thinnest silver gauze
had been thrown over it. The canopy of heaven had a clear
and sparkling appearance, while the horizon was on all sides
thickly studded with ice-islands, whose clustering peaks appeared to penetrate the airy clouds.

> Silence accompanied : for beast and bird,
> They to their *icy* couch, these to their nests
> Were slunk.

But to attempt describing the grandeur of a moonlight-scene
in the ice would be vain indeed. No language (at least that
I could select) would afford adequate means of description.
The richest proves but poor in the attempt ; and all the pos-

sible combination of words are few indeed to those of nature, under all her variety of forms and colours. In a short time we regained our vessel, when we retired, much gratified with our evening's amusement.

Monday, July the 20th. Weather continues very fine, sky serene and calm; the horizon is covered on all sides with ice, consisting for the most part of broken-up fields. About twelve o'clock a light fair breeze sprung up, when the captain gave orders to have more sail set. A person unaccustomed to the navigation of these seas, would consider it as altogether impossible that a ship could make any way when completely beset with ice: still, however, when the breeze is fair, and the flakes of ice not very large, it is astonishing what progress she will make in the course of twenty-four hours. During this operation of forcing through the ice, every man on board has his place assigned him, while the captain takes his in the most convenient one for observing when the ship approaches very near the piece of ice directly a-head; immediately on the word being given, the ship is put about, and in less than a minute is moving in a quite contrary direction. When a " vein of water,"* as they term it, presents itself, they always endeavour to avail themselves of it.

Tuesday, July the 20th. Weather continues very fine, wind fair; forcing our way through huge masses of ice: about two o'clock, the breeze dying away, we got fastened to one of the principal icebergs. This island, I am certain, could not be less than 300 feet high, and about a quarter of a mile in circumference. The anchors which they use on these occasions resemble very much an italic *S*; to one extremity a cable is attached, while a hole is made in the ice for the purpose of receiving the other. Being now completely at rest, we had more leisure and more inclination to contemplate the very grand and novel scene with which we were surrounded. The first thing that engages the attention of the passing mariner, is the majestic, as well as singular forms which the ice assumes in these chilling regions. I have seen many of these immense masses bear a very close resemblance to an ancient abbey with arched doors and windows, and all the rich embroidery of the Gothic style of architecture; while others assume the appearance of

---

* Navigating among icebergs in the gloom of night, has sometimes been attended with fatal consequences. Occurring far from land, and in unexpected situations, the danger would be extreme, were they not providentially rendered visible by their natural effulgence, which enables the mariner to distinguish them at some distance, even in the darkest night, or during the prevalence of the densest fog.—*See Scoresby on Polar Ice.*

a Grecian temple, supported by round massive columns of an azure hue, which at a distance looked like the purest mountain granite. These stupendous masses, or icebergs, as they are termed, are some of them the creation of ages, and receive annually additional height by the falling of snows and rain, which instantly congeal, and in this way more than repair the loss occasioned by the influence of the melting sun. The spray of the ocean, which dashes against these mountains, freezes into an infinite variety of forms, and gives to the spectator ideal towers, streets, churches, steeples, and, in fact, every shape which the most romantic imagination could picture to itself. When, at the close of evening, the almost level beams of the descending sun are directed on the numerous apertures, or chambers, as we might suppose them, of these imaginary palaces, abbeys, &c. the effect is inconceivably grand: in one place you see them touched with a rich golden colour; in another, with a light purple tint; and in others, again, with a rich crimson suffusion.

Some of these islands, as I have already mentioned, remain stationary for ages in this frozen climate; while the smaller masses, or *floating mountains*, as they are called, move slowly and majestically along, chilling the ambient atmosphere for miles around, until, being drifted into southern latitudes, they are gradually dissolved in the boundless element. It sometimes happens, that two of these masses, though distinct* above water, are intimately united beneath its surface. I recollect the captain mentioning to me, that owing to this circumstance, the Hudson's Bay Company, a few years ago, lost one of their finest vessels. The master, not supposing but that they were quite distinct beneath, ran the vessel in between them; the ship immediately foundered, and every person on board would have perished, but that fortunately another of the company's ships was at hand to take them up.

By a *field of ice* is to be understood one uninterrupted sheet of considerable extent. They vary from one to many leagues in length. Mr. Scoresby states, that upon one which he saw he conceived a coach might be driven a hundred miles without meeting with any obstruction. This I have not the smallest

---

* Barentz, and the famous Dutch navigator Heemskerk, in their voyage for the discovery of a north-east passage, after wintering at Nova Zembla, lost their ship in this way, and then sailed many hundred leagues in an open boat, through the ice; during which, they were often assaulted by the white bears, and sometimes obliged to drag the boat and all its lading a good way over the ice. They came at last to Kotira, in Lapland, where they were taken up by a Dutch vessel.—*See Crantz' Greenland.*

doubt to be the fact. Indeed, I have frequently gone aloft myself for the purpose of ascertaining their extent, but have often been unable, as far as the eye could reach, to observe even a single fissure in them. On their surface, which is generally raised three or four feet above the level of the water, I have seen the seals bark and frolic in hundreds. The coalition of two of these great fields produces a most singular phenomenon; the larger forces the lesser out of the water, and adds it to its surface; and in this way a second and a third are often superadded, until the whole forms an aggregate of a tremendous height. The collision of the greater fields is often attended with a noise, that for a time deprives you of the power of hearing any thing else, resembling very much the sound of distant thunder: the meeting of the smaller pieces produces a harsh grinding kind of noise, not unlike, as Mr. Scoresby accurately remarks, that of complicated machinery.

During the summer months these masses become very brittle, and frequently give way with a tremendous report, in this way laying the foundation for other islands similar to themselves. At this time considerable risk is incurred, either by going *ashore* on them, as we may term it, or by allowing the vessel to approach too near their perpendicular front. It has not unfrequently happened that ships have been sunk by their detached portions falling in on the deck. That these apprehensions are not imaginary, the following circumstance will, I think, afford a satisfactory proof.

One morning I went out with a party of the men in the jolly-boat, for the purpose of towing away the vessel from one of these ice-bergs, in order to guard against the accident to which I have just alluded. In this instance the island was so high, that its summit stretched in an arched form for a considerable distance over the top-mast of the vessel. Before getting to that part of the island to which the ice-anchor was attached, it was necessary to pass a projecting point, where the island, as it were, *shelved* out to a considerable distance. The man who had the command of the boat, unwilling to lose time, instead of sailing round this projecting portion, ordered the boat to be rowed directly under it. We had scarcely got half-way when a violent report,* like that of a piece of artillery, an-

---

* Ice-bergs, on being struck with an axe for the purpose of placing a mooring anchor, have been known to rend asunder, and precipitate the careless seaman into the watery chasm; whilst, occasionally, the masses are hurled apart and fall, in contrary directions, with a prodigious crash, bury-

nounced to us that a part of the island was about to give way. Every one appeared in the greatest alarm. The boatswain ordered the boat to be pushed off instantly. Before, however, we could get completely free of the ice, the whole side of the mountain was detached with a noise like thunder, and instantly we were immersed in the yawning gulph, from which we never expected to rise again ; in a few seconds, however, our little jolly-boat rose triumphant on the ridge of the foaming wave. Having cleared out the fragments of ice which had got into the boat, we made towards the ship, where we were welcomed as if we had risen from the dead. After changing our clothes and taking some refreshment, we soon forgot this nearly fatal occurrence. The violent noise which those dinuptions, or *icequakes*, as they are very appropriately termed, produces, is not, as Mr. Lesslie remarks, to be altogether attributed to the crash of the falling fragments. " In those frightful climates," observes this ingenious philosopher, " the winter at once sets in with most intense frost, which probably envelopes the globules of air, separated from the water in the act of congelation, and, invading them on all sides, reduces them to a state of high condensation. When the mild weather begins, therefore, to prevail, the body of ice, penetrated by the warmth, becomes soft and friable; and the minute, but. numerously interspersed globules of imprisoned air, exerting together their concentrated elasticity, produce the most violent explosive dinuptions."—*See* Lesslie *on Heat and Moisture.*

With regard to the manner in which those mountains and fields of ice are formed, I do not propose entering into any lengthened discussion ; and this I conceive the more unnecessary, as Mr. Scoresby's late ingenious and very able publication contains almost every thing that can be said on this obscure, though very interesting subject. I propose condensing the few remarks I have to make into as narrow and as simple a form as possible.

The greater part of the difficulties and principal source of obscurity in the numerous discussions which have taken place on this subject, appear to me to turn on this single point: Can ice be formed on the surface of sea-water ?—For my part, I can conceive no reason whatever why it should not.

ing boats and men in one common ruin. The awful effect produced by a solid mass, many thousands of tons in weight, changing its situation with the velocity of a falling body, whereby its aspiring summit is in a moment buried in the ocean, can be more easily imagined than described.—*See* Scoresby *on Polar Ice. Transactions of the* Wernerian Society.

The circumstances which appear to me to favour its production, I shall arrange under the following heads:

First, Intense cold.

Second, A state of rest,

Third, The falling of crystallized snow and hail-stones.

Fourth, The separation of ice from the bottom of the ocean.

And first, with regard to intense cold, Any one at all acquainted with these rigorous climes must allow, that there is here an abundance of this the most essential of all requisites. During the winter season, which usually continues for nine months, the spirit thermometer is commonly found to stand at 50. Quicksilver freezes into a solid mass; consequently, the cold which then prevails must exceed 71 degrees, or 39 below the commencement of Fahrenheit's scale; a degree of natural cold which, I believe, is rarely exceeded, Wine, and even ardent spirits,* become converted into a spongy mass of ice; even the "living forests" do not escape, the very sap of the trees being frozen; and which, owing to the internal expansion which takes place in consequence, occasionally burst with tremendous noise,

Now it is proved by experiments, that when the thermometer falls to 27°, other circumstances being favourable, that a pellicle of ice will be formed on the surface of sea-water. How then, I would ask, is the excess of cold between 27 and 50, exerting itself? Are we to suppose that it floats passively along the chilled surface of the ocean without exerting any frigorific influence? This would be in direct opposition to one of the most generally established laws of caloric, that of diffusing itself among bodies until an equilibrium of temperature is established. But it may be said, that no ice can be formed until the whole mass of fluid is reduced to the temperature of 35°,† or that point at which sea-water begins to expand, If, however, this intense cold continues a sufficient length of time to affect the entire body of fluid, this objection must, I conceive, fall to the ground. Now, any one who considers for a moment the duration of the tedious and dreary Arctic winter, must, I should think, allow that there is more than sufficient time for the whole mass to become cooled down considerably below this temperature. This effect will of course be much more

---

* By this I mean, of course, common spirits.

† I have said 35°, presuming that sea-water will begin to expand the same number of degrees above its freezing point that common water does; but of this I am not certain.

C 2

readily produced in those seas that have not free access to the main body of the ocean, as also where the depth is not very great. It may also be said, that owing to the currents and heaving tides by which they are agitated, the different portions of water are so effectually intermixed as, in some degree, to equalize the temperature. It must be observed, however, that this equilibrium of temperature by no means takes place with such rapidity as we should, *a priori*, suppose. In proof of this I may adduce the well-known fact, that the temperature of the sea always falls in shoal-water; hence the thermometer has been found a very useful instrument in navigation, being frequently substituted for the more tedious process of sounding. It may be also observed, that fluids are very bad conductors of caloric, and that, as these seas are never agitated by very high winds, the excess of cold will readily counteract the influence which the currents might otherwise produce.

The second circumstance which I have to notice, as being highly favourable for the production of ice, is a state of rest. Every one who has visited these remote regions must have noticed at once the remarkable stillness of the northern seas. It is, in fact, as smooth and as unruffled as the most retired harbour, owing, I should suppose, to the enormous pressure which the ice already formed exerts on its surface.* Mr. Scoresby tells us, that the ice, by its weight, can keep down the most violent surges, and that its resistance is so effectual, that ships sheltered by it rarely find the sea disturbed by swells. This state of rest will, I conceive, favour the production of ice in the same way as it does other kinds of crystallization; namely, by allowing the particles held in solution to arrange themselves at determinate angles. Lest, however, it should be looked on as a kind of *petitio principii*, to argue in favour of the production of ice from an effect produced by ice already formed, I proceed to state the third source to which I have alluded; namely, the falling of crystallized snow and hail-stones. These, I conceive, may operate in two ways: First, by the mechanical agitation which they give to the surface of the ocean, thus acting in the same way as in the common experiment of immersing a portion of water contained

---

* All these phenomena exactly accord with the system of philosophy lately promulgated by Sir Richard Phillips, who ascribes all phenomena to aggregate and atomic motion; and the frozen state of the Polar seas to the diminished rotatory motion of the aggregate, as well as the diffusion of the solar light, or atomic motion of light, over the oblique surface.

                                                            Editor.

in a glass tube into a freezing moisture; if kept at perfect
rest, no crystallization will take place, at least not until the
entire mass is reduced to a very low degree of temperature;
but if slightly agitated, as by striking the side of the tube with
a piece of money, the whole instantly starts into a solid mass.
Secondly, by serving as so many nuclei, from which crystallization will spread on all sides; thus operating, I conceive, on
the same principle as the crystal of a salt does when dropped
into a saline solution. Mr. Kerwan was the first, I believe,
who remarked, that when a crystal of the same kind of salt
with that held in solution was dropped in, the process of
crystallization went on still more rapidly. Now, crystallized
snow and hail-stones, being merely small portions of congealed
water, may, perhaps, operate in a similar way.*

To the sources already enumerated, I have lastly to add,
that of the formation of ice at the bottom of the ocean, and
which becoming detached by the force of the currents, will,
by its diminished and specific gravity, rise to the surface and
become, as it were, a centre for further accumulations. From
the difficulties attendant on an explanation of this curious
phenomenon, some have considered it as altogether improba-
ble, while others have gone the length of denying it altogether. The circumstance however, at least with regard to fresh
water, is now put beyond the possibility of all doubt, and we
can very readily conceive, that what a lesser, degree of cold
will effect in the beds of lakes and rivers, a still greater will
be able to accomplish at the bottom of the ocean. Mr. Lesslie,
in a note prefixed to his very interesting work on the subject
of heat, tells us, that many of the rivers in Siberia and Swit-
zerland are found to have their beds lined, during the greater
part of the year, with a thick crust of ice. Saussure describes
a similar appearance in the lakes of Geneva. Mr. Garnet, in
a very interesting paper contained in the last number of the
Journal of Science and of Arts, gives a very minute account
of this singular appearance. He mentions one place, in particular, where this phenomenon is to be observed in a very
striking manner. As the very valuable publication, in which
this interesting paper is contained, is in the hands of few, except scientific readers, I trust an account of it will not be
deemed superfluous.

---

* When, observes Mr. Lesslie, we examine the stricture of a hail-stone,
we shall perceive a snowy kernel incased by a harder crust. It has very
nearly the appearance of a drop of water suddenly frozen, the particles of
air being driven from the surface towards the centre, where they form a
spongy texture.—*See* Lesslie *on Heat and Moisture.*

On the river Wharfe, near Otley, in the West Riding of Yorkshire, is a weir, or mill-dam, the structure of which is of hewn stone, forming a plane, inclined to an angle of from 35° to 50° fronting the north, and extending from W. to E. to the length of 250 or 300 yards. When the wind suddenly shifts from S.W. to N. W., and blows with great impetuosity, accompanied with severe frost and heavy falls of snow, the stone which composes the weir soon becomes encrusted with ice, which increases so rapidly in thickness, as in a short time to impede the course of the stream that falls over it in a tolerable uniform sheet, and with considerable velocity : at the same time the wind, blowing strongly from the N. W. contributes to repel the water, and freeze such as adheres to the crust of ice when its surface comes nearly in contact with the air. The consequence is, that in a short time the current is entirely obstructed, and the superincumbent water forced to a higher level. But, as the above-mentioned causes continue to act, the ice is also elevated by a perpetual aggregation of particles; till, by a series of similar operations, an icy-mound, or barrier, is formed so high as to force the water over the opposite shore, and thus produce an apparent inundation. But in a short time the accumulated weight of a great many thousand cubic feet of water presses so strongly against the barrier, as to burst a passage through some weak part, through which the water escapes, and subsides to its former level, leaving the singular appearance of a wall or rampart of ice, three or four feet in thickness, along the greatest part of the upper edge of the weir. The ice composing this barrier, where it adheres to the stone, is of a solid consistency, but the upper part consists of a multitude of thin laminæ, or layers, resting upon each other in a confused manner, and at different angles of inclination, their interstices being occupied by innumerable spiculæ diverging and crossing each other in all directions. The whole mass resembles in its texture the white and porous ice, which may be seen at the edge of a pond, or small rill, where the water has subsided during a frost."—*See Journal of Science and Arts. No. X.*

The explanation of this curious phenomena is certainly very difficult, and would appear to argue somewhat against the long-received opinion of the diminished specific gravity of water after being cooled down beyond the temperature of 39. As there has been as yet no satisfactory theory offered on the subject, I shall beg leave to state, in very few words, in what manner I conceive this deposition to take place. While reading Dr. Garnet's paper, I was very forcibly struck with the peculiar circumstances in which he states this icy incrustation to take place : thus he tells us, that it is always formed in greatest abundance in proportion to the magnitude and number of the stones composing the bed of the river, combined with the velocity of the current; as also that it abounds most in *rough* and rapid places, and not at all where mud or clay is deposited. Now it has occurred to me, that, perhaps, the formation of ice in these situations may be owing to the same causes that gave rise to the deposition of dew and hoarfrost on grass, twigs, and other *fibrous* substances; namely, by their possessing a greater radiating power. The *rough end* surfaces of the stones I conceive to operate in the same way as the vegetable fibres do in a clear, unclouded atmosphere, by allowing the " affluent" wave to come in closer proximity with the surface, and thus facilitate the discharge of caloric from the bed of the river. That none appears where mud and earth are deposited, I should suppose to be owing to their presenting a smooth surface, in consequence of the water constantly rippling over it; thus the stratum of incumbent fluid is prevented coming into as close contact as if it presented a ruggid surface. Just in the same way as if we were to take a highly-polished vessel of silver and fill it with hot water ; it will take, suppose twenty minutes, to cool a certain number of degrees; but if its surface be scratched with sand-paper, it will cool the same number *of degrees* in nearly half the time. That a great part of the effect is owing, in this case, to the number of projecting points is proved by the circumstance of simply scratching it in an opposite direction, when the effect is considerably lessened : the number of projecting points being thus diminished, it will now take a much longer time to cool down the same number of degrees. It is on the same principle that a thin covering of muslin, instead of preventing the escape of heat, as *à priori* we should suppose, does actually favour its discharge. The N. W. wind may act in two ways : first, by its greater degree of cold ; secondly, perhaps, being less impregnated with the particles of foreign bodies, in consequence of passing over the frozen regions of the north, it may be thus more favourably circumstanced for the escape and transmission of those calorific radiations.

The *rays* act on the same principle as a clear unclouded sky does in producing the deposition of the aqueous meteors already alluded to. The only way, however, of ascertaining this would be by trying what effect screens of different kinds would produce, when interposed between the surface of the water and the strong current of the N. W. wind. This explanation appears to me to be supported by a fact long since observed, that water will congeal, though the ambient air should

be several degrees above the freezing point. The effect is, no
doubt, considerably hastened by the cold produced by evaporation from the surface. This, however, exerts a very limited
influence ; for, after it has arrived at a certain temperature, the " shell of air" which comes in contact with it,
before making any ascensional effort, will discharge a quantity
of its surplus heat, and thus preserve the temperature of the
fluid within certain limits. Something similar to this may be
observed while passing through the fields of a cool evening.
We often observe dew, or hoar-frost, deposited on twigs, grass,
and other substances, though the air, even a few inches above
their surface, is several degrees above temperature. With regard to the uses which this singular phenomenon may serve :
—perhaps, in consequence of the heat extricated during the
process of congelation, it may thus prevent the temperature of
the numerous organized bodies, contained in those situations,
from being reduced to a degree which would be incompa-
tible with their healthy functions. It will thus render those
substances the same services as the deposition of dew and hoar-
frost does to the tender plants, the caloric, given out during
these processes, preserving them from the cool air which is so
prevalent during our summer evenings.

It will in all probability be objected to the suggestions I
have here thrown out, that they are in direct opposition to the
observations of Mr. Lesslie, who asserts, that when the Can-
nister Reflector and Differential Thermometer were plunged
into water, that no radiation can be observed; and hence this
ingenious philosopher concludes, that no radiation will take
place, except when the radiating body is surrounded with an
elastic medium. I may remark, however, that the experiments
which he adduces in support of this opinion, are by no means
decisive of the point. Substances cool so rapidly, when
plunged into water, that there is scarcely time for the differential thermometer to be affected ; and, besides, the heat could
scarcely accumulate in the foral-ball, in such quantity as to
occasion a sensible rise. Moreover, I can see no reason whatever why radiant caloric should not pass through water as well
as air. They are both fluids ; they receive and transmit slow
communicating caloric in a precisely similar way, namely, by
a constant recession or migration of heated particles; they
agree in many of their chemical relations, such as exterior
solvent power, &c. ; they also agree in possessing elasticity ;
though water is by no means susceptible of the same degree
of condensation as air : still, however, that it possesses this
property, in a slight degree, is obvious, from the common
amusement in which boys indulge, of projecting a stone forci-

bly on the surface of a pond, thus making what they call a duck and drake. Agreeing, then, as these two fluids do in so many particulars, what is there, I would ask, in the constitution of water that should prevent the transmission of radiant caloric?—Besides, if not transmitted through this fluid, what then becomes of it? is it converted into slow communicating caloric? This would be to assert their identity, which, I believe, all philosophers deny. Finally, I may remark, that the entire of this subject, notwithstanding the ingenious and laborious experiments of Mr. Lesslie, appears to me involved in a good deal of obscurity. The nature of radiant heat; whether identical with light or not; as also the causes, why one portion of caloric should escape by radiation, and another by slow communication; these are points on which, I think, we still stand much in need of further information. Until, therefore, these matters are more fully investigated, I conceive we have just grounds to conclude, that water and air bear the same relations to radiant caloric.

Having now enumerated the various causes which I conceive to favour the formation of ice on sea-water, I have further to remark, that this opinion is supported by the actual observations of several very intelligent navigators. Mr. M'Nairne, in 1776, shewed that, when Fahrenheit's thermometer is at 27½ degrees, the fresh particles of sea-water will freeze, and leave nothing but strong brine behind.

Barentz saw the sea, at Nova Zembla, suddenly frozen over to the depth of several inches.

Mr. Scoresby, the intelligent navigator already mentioned, tells us, that he has seen ice grow on the surface of the sea to a consistence capable of stopping the progress of a ship with a brisk wind, even when exposed to the waves of the north sea and western ocean. The first layer, or *slush* ice, as it is termed, being once formed, there is, I conceive, but little difficulty in accounting for their subsequent enlargement. When the winter season sets in, and that crystallized* snow begins to fall, it becomes consolidated by the excessive cold of the climate, and will, of course, press down the primary strata, to use a geological phrase. The other aqueous meteors of hail, rain, &c. suffering a similar condensation, we can readily conceive, that, by a gradual accumulation in this

---

* That snow is deposited on the ice in high northern latitudes must be allowed, because no field has yet been met with which did not support a considerable burthen of it.—*See Scoresby on Polar Ice.—Wernerian Transactions.*

way, masses of any size may be formed. The disruptions so
common during the summer months, as also the overlapping
of the fields, will likewise lay the foundation for further accumulations. The cause assigned by Mr. Lesslie will also assist
in accounting for their progressive increase. " The most satisfactory mode," remarks this able philosopher, " of explain-
ing the phenomenon, is to refer it to the operation of a general
principle, by which the inequalities on the surface of a field
of ice must be constantly increased. The lower parts of the
field being nearer the tempered mass of the ocean, are not so
cold as those which project into the atmosphere, and, consequently, the air which ascends, becoming chilled in sweeping
over the eminences, there deposits some of its moisture, forming an icy coat. But this continued incrustation, in the lapse
of ages, produces a vast accumulation, till the shapeless mass
is at length precipitated by its own weight."

With regard to the kind of solution which the field-ice
affords, a variety of opinions have prevailed. Some asserting
that the solution had a saline taste, others, that it was quite
free from it. This discordancy may, I conceive, be explained
in this way: when the saline substances dissolved in sea-
water lose their medium of solution, it is obvious they must
be precipitated; and even though some of the particles should
continue interspersed through the frozen mass, it must be
merely in a state of mechanical union. The superincumbent
layer of water, however, by slowly percolating through the
spongy mass, will gradually wash away those entangled particles. We can thus very readily account for the circumstance
of even the portion which is formed from sea-water affording
a solution* altogether destitute of saline taste. When, however, this process of filtration is arrested by the deposition of
an incumbent layer of *fresh-water* ice, which is of a very close
texture, these masses will then have a saline taste.

Professor Lesslie, of Edinburgh, who has thrown much
light on this very interesting department of physical science,
has lately discovered the singular fact, that frigorific impressions are constantly showering down during the day as well
as during the night from the higher regions of the atmosphere.
From a variety of experiments performed by this philosopher,
for the purpose of measuring those pulsations, it appears that
the effect varies considerably according to the condition of
the higher regions; it is greatest while the sky has the pure

---

* I have brought large fragments on board; have melted them, and uniformly found that the solution was altogether free from the taste of salt-
water.

azure hue ; it diminishes fast, as the atmosphere becomes loaded with spreading clouds; and it is almost extinguished when low fogs settle on the surface. These effects are, no doubt, more conspicuous in the finer regions of the globe. Accordingly, they did not escape the observation of the ancients, but gave rise to opinions which were embodied in the language of poetry. The term Ἀήρ, was applied only to the grossest part of the atmosphere, while the highest portion of it, free from clouds and vapour, and bordering on the pure fields of æther, received the kindred appellation of Αἰθρία. In southern climates especially, a transpiercing cold is felt at night under the clear and sparkling canopy of heaven. The natives carefully avoid exposing themselves to this supposed celestial influence, yet a thin shed of palm-leaves may be sufficient at once to screen them from the scorching rays of the sun, and to shelter them against the chilling impressions rained from the higher atmosphere. The captains of the French gallies in the Mediterranean used formerly to cool their wines in summer by hanging their flasks all night from the masts. At day-break they were taken down, and lapped in several folds of flannel, to preserve them in the same state. The frigorific impression of a serene and azure sky must undoubtedly have concurred with the power of evaporation in augmenting the energy of the process of nocturnal cooling, practised anciently in Egypt, and now systematically pursued in the higher grounds of India. As the chilliness accumulated on the ground is greatest in clear nights, when the moon shines brightest, it seemed very natural to impute this effect partly to some influence emanating from that feeble luminary.

The instrument which Professor Lesslie employed in his experiment on this highly interesting subject, he terms an Æthrioscope (from the Greek word Αἰθρίος, which, in reference to the atmosphere, signifies at once *clear, dry*, and *cold*.) It is, in fact, a combination of the ordinary pyroscope, and is formed by adapting that instrument to the cavity of a polished metallic cup, of rather an oblong spheroidal shape, the axis being occupied by the sentient ball, while the section of a horizontal plane, passing through the upper, forms the orifice. The cup may be made of thin brass, or silver, either hammered or cast, and then turned and polished on a lathe, the diameter being from two to four inches, and the eccentricity of the elliptical figure varied within certain limits, according to circumstances; the most convenient proportion, however, is to have this eccentricity equal to half the transverse axis, and consequently to place the focus at the third part of the whole height of the cavity, the diameter of the sentient ball being likewise nearly the third part of that of the orifice of the cup. In order to separate more the balls of the pyroscope, the gilt one may be carried somewhat higher than the other, and lodged in the swell of the cavity, its stem being bent to the curve, and the neck partially widened to prevent the risk of dividing the coloured liquor in carriage. A lid of the same thin unpolished metal as the cup itself, is fitted to the mouth of the æthrioscope, and only removed when an observation is to be made. The scale may extend to sixty or seventy millesimal degrees above the zero, and about fifteen degrees below it. Should Mr. L.'s anticipations with regard to the utility of this instrument prove to be well grounded, it will prove to be a valuable acquisition indeed to every physical cabinet. The æthrioscope, remarks this fascinating writer, thus opens new scenes to our view. It extends its sensation through indefinite space, and reveals the condition of the remotest atmosphere. Constructed with still greater delicacy, it may, perhaps, scent the distant winds, and detect the actual temperature of every quarter of the heavens. The impressions of cold which arrive from the north will probably be found stronger than those received from the south. But the instrument has yet been scarcely tried. We are anxious to compare its indications for the course of a whole year, and still more solicitous to receive its reports from other climates, and brighter skies.—*See Supplement to the Encyclopædia Britannica, Articles Climate and Cold. Also, Transactions of the Royal Society of Edinburgh,* vol. vii. part ii.

I have been induced to dwell thus long on the proofs which I conceive may be offered in favour of the opinion that the surface of the northern seas is annually subjected to the process of congellation, as on this single circumstance, in a great measure, depends the success of the northern expedition; for if these seas are, as I have endeavoured to prove, annually exposed to the eternal fluctuation of having their surface frozen over, they must for ever present to the intrepid navigator obstacles altogether insurmountable.*

---

* The reason, I conceive, why so large a body of ice has been detached from the west coast of Greenland is simply this: In consequence of the number of bays, creeks, and inlets, which the coast of Greenland presents, ice will very readily be formed, and will, owing to the shelter which the land affords, in course of time accumulate to an enormous extent. At length, however, from agitation, or from their great weight overcoming the power of cohesion, the key-stone of the mass gives way; the icy chains which held these frightful masses are dissolved, and the whole is gradually drifted into southern latitudes.

Wednesday, July the 21st. A party of us went out on the ice for the purpose of amusing ourselves. We had not walked far when we discovered several ponds of very fine fresh water. Having sent intelligence of this to the captain, he immediately ordered out some of the men to fill the water-casks. It not only tasted very well, but answered admirably for every culinary purpose. In some of these ponds we observed a small fish, to which they give the name of Miller's Thumbs.

Thursday, the 22d. Availing ourselves of a fair wind, which sprung up this morning, we took in the ice-anchors, and set sail in company with our consorts.

Two o'clock, P. M. Forcing our way through very heavy ice, got several very severe knocks. Obliged to keep the pumps going day and night.

Friday, July 23d. Still forcing our way through the ice ; wind fair ; weather uncommonly fine.

Saturday, July 24th. The breeze has nearly died away; weather continues fine. About twelve o'clock we got anchored to an island of ice. Lost sight of the George. Fired a gun, which was answered in a few minutes. The captain supposes them to be about a league a-head.

Sunday, 25th. The George having made a signal for getting under way, we loosed our anchors, and set sail. In about an hour we got up with her.

—— This day, while sailing through straggling ice, one of the men on the quarter-deck observed, at a few yards distance, a silver bear and her two young cubs. The captain immediately ordered the jolly-boat to be lowered, and muskets, pistols, cutlasses, &c. to be got in readiness. All things being prepared, Mr. Fidler, Mr. Cockerell, the first mate, with one or two more, set, out in pursuit of them. We were all leaning over the deck, waiting with the greatest anxiety for the interesting scene that we expected to witness. They had not got many yards from the vessel, when I beheld a very affecting sight : the mother, observing their approach, and aware of their intention, set up a most doleful cry, and presently clasped her two young ones within her two fore-paws. First she would look at one, then at another, and again resume her piteous cry. Perceiving the men to approach still nearer, she got them on her back, and dived under water to a considerable distance ; when exhausted, she made to the ice for shelter. This she did several successive times. The gentlemen who went out for the purpose of shooting her, were so justly affected at the sight, that they humanely returned to the ship without discharging their muskets. Still, however, the poor bear apprehended danger. After getting on a detached piece of ice, she again clasped her young ones with the greatest tenderness, and continued her heart-melting cries! In about ten minutes, another party,* not subject to the same correct sensibility as the former, went in pursuit of her. Immediately on observing this, she again took her young on her back; one time, getting under water, at another, escaping to the ice for refuge. When the party had got within a short distance of her, they all fired. The mother, however, had covered her young cubs so effectually, that she alone was wounded; one of the balls entered her chest. The scene that followed was, if possible, still more affecting than that we had already witnessed.

Though mortally wounded, she retained within her fond embraces her tender young. It looked as though the iron grasp of death could not tear asunder those ties of affection which bound her to them. Still she would fondly gaze at one, then at another, occasionally renewing her piteous cries, which had now become much more feeble. But the purple current of life was ebbing fast through the wound : her sides heaved—her eye became glassy and dim—she looked at her young ones—gave a convulsive sob—laid down her head, and expired !†

After this, they had no difficulty in taking the young cubs. They in vain, however, endeavoured to loose them from their parent's embraces. Even while dragging her up the side of the vessel, they still kept their hold. When they had got her on board, she was immediately skinned.‡ When the skin was removed, they put it into the cage which had been prepared for the young cubs. As they roared most hideously from the time they were torn from the mother, we were in hopes that this might pacify them; and it did so : it was no sooner introduced, than they laid their heads down on it, and growled in a very affecting manner. When any one attempted to touch it, they roared very loud, and appeared much more irrit-

---

* It might be added, of monsters in the shape of men, or human savages! —EDITOR.

† The monsters engaged in this transaction merit the torments of the damned—the curses of men—and the vengeance of an insulted Deity.— EDITOR.

‡ On examining the wound, I found the ball had passed through the arch of the aorta, and had lodged in the intercostal muscles of the opposite side. I cut out the parts, and immersed them in a bottle filled with spirits; but one of the crew, an unfortunate Irishman, got hold of it in some way or other, and being fonder of whiskey than morbid anatomy, drank the fluid in which I had them preserved, and thus spoiled my preparation.

able than usual. They were brought home, and sold in London at a very high price.*

When detached from its young, how very different is the character of the polar bear from that I have just described. It is then a most formidable animal, being apparently the natural lord of those frozen regions. Every other animal shudders at his approach, considering it as the signal for immediate destruction. The seals either retire to their submarine dwellings, or conceal themselves in the crevices of the ice-islands; while the bear, stalking along with solemn majesty, " faces the breeze, raises his head, and snuffs the passing scent, whereby he discovers the nearest route to his odorous banquet." A favourite poet, with great truth and beauty, thus describes the march of this formidable animal :—

" There, through the piny forest, half absorbed,
Rough tenant of those shades, the shapeless bear,
With dangling ice, all horrid, stalks forlorn ;
Slow-paced, and sourer as the storms increase,
He makes his bed beneath the inclement drift,
And with stern patience, scorning weak complaint,
Hardens his heart against assailing want."

They are possessed of such uncommon strength, and defend themselves, when beset, with such extraordinary obstinacy, that even the natives of the country never venture to attack them but in parties of eight or ten, and even then are often defeated with the loss of one or more of their number. Though to a skilful rifleman the danger is very much diminished, the bear is still an animal of tremendous strength and fierceness, as will appear from the following adventure.— Captain Lewis tells us, that one evening the men in the hindmost of the canoes discovered a large silver bear lying in the open grounds, about 300 paces from the river. Six of them, all good hunters, set out to attack him, and concealing themselves by a small eminence, came unperceived within forty paces of him. Four of them now fired, and each lodged a ball in his body; two of them directly through the lungs. The justly-enraged animal sprung up, and ran open-mouthed

---

* The great attachment which the she-bear has for her young, is well known to the American hunter. No danger can induce her to abandon them. Even when they are sufficiently grown to be able to climb a tree, her anxiety for their safety is but little diminished. At that time, if hunted, her first care is to make her young climb to a place of safety. If they shew any reluctance, she beats them, and having succeeded, turns fearlessly on her pursuers. Perhaps, in the animal economy, maternal affection is almost always commensurate with the helplessness of the young.
See Bradbury's Travels in America.

at them. As he came near, the two hunters who had reserved
their fire gave him two wounds, one of which breaking his
shoulder, retarded his motion for a moment; but before they
could reload he was so near that they were obliged to run to
the river, and before they reached it he had almost overtaken
them. Two jumped into the canoe, the other four separated,
and concealing themselves in the willows, fired as fast as each
could load. They struck him several times, but they only
exasperated him; and he at last pursued two of them so
closely, that they jumped down a perpendicular bank of
twenty feet into the river; the bear sprang after them, and
was within a few feet of the hindmost, when one of the hunters
on shore shot him in the head, and killed him. They dragged
him to the shore, and found that eight balls had passed through
his body in different directions.

Barentz, in his voyage in search of a north-east passage to
China, had melancholy proofs of the ferocity of these animals
in the island of Nova Zembla, where they attacked his men,
seizing them in their mouths, carrying them off, and devouring them in sight of their comrades. " On the 6th of September," observes this interesting writer, " some sailors again
landed to seek for a certain sort of stone, a species of dia-
mond, of which a sufficient quantity is also found in the Isle
of Slates. During this search, two of the sailors, sleeping by
one another, a white bear, very lean, approached them softly,
and seized one by the nape of the neck. The sailor, not
knowing what it was, cried out, ' Who has seized me thus
behind?' His companion, having raised his head, said, ' Hol-
loa! my dear friend, it is a bear!' and immediately rising,
ran away. The bear bit the unfortunate man in several parts
of the head, and having quite mangled it, sucked the blood.
The rest of the persons who were on shore, to the number of
twenty, immediately ran with their firelocks and pikes, and
found the bear devouring the body. On seeing the men, he
ran towards them with incredible fury, threw himself upon
one of them, carried him away, and tore him to pieces, which
so terrified them that they all fled. Those who remained in
the vessel, seeing them thus flee, and return towards the shore,
jumped into the boats, and rowed with all their force to receive them. When they had landed, and beheld this lament-
able spectacle, they encouraged the others to return with them
to the combat, that all together they might attack this ferocious animal. Three of them advanced a little, the bear still
continuing to devour his prey, without being at all disturbed
at the sight of thirty men so near him. The two pilots having
fired three times without hitting the animal, the purser ad-

THE POLAR BEAR.

vanced a little further, and shot the bear in the head, close by the eye, which did not cause him to quit his prey; but holding the body always by the neck, which he was devouring, carried it away as yet almost quite entire. Nevertheless, they then perceived that he began to totter; and the purser going towards him, with a Scotchman, they gave him several sabre wounds, without his abandoning his prey. At length the pilot Geyser, having given him a violent blow with the butt-end of his firelock on the muzzle, which brought him to the ground, the purser leaped upon him, and cut his throat. The two bodies, half devoured, were interred in the Isle of the Slates, and the skin of the bear was carried to Amsterdam."

Frequently they attack, and even attempt to board armed vessels, at a great distance from the shore, and are sometimes repelled with great difficulty. While on land they prey on foxes, hares, martins, and young birds; they also eat various kinds of berries, which they may chance to find while ranging through the trackless desert. During these excursions they not unfrequently enter the habitations of the natives, and carry off one of the party. Mr. Howes, one of the inland governors, mentioned to me, that one evening he and his companions were sitting in their wigwam enjoying a social hour after a hard day's hunting, when, on a sudden, they found one of their party to disappear. A white bear had, in fact, carried him off by the skirts of his coat. They all immediately sallied out in pursuit of him, which, when the bear observed, he instantly dropped his prey and made off into the woods. It is said that the best mode of repelling them, on these occasions, is by the smell of burnt feathers. During the summer months, being allured by the scent of the carcases of whales, seals, &c. they venture out on the ice. They have been seen on some of those islands at the distance of more than eighty miles from land, preying and feeding as they float along. During the winter they retire and immerse themselves deep beneath the snow; here they pass the long and dreary arctic winter, and do not again appear until the return of spring.

The whole animal is white except the point of the nose, and the claws, which are of a deep black colour; the ears are rather small and sharp; the eyes small and of a deep jet-black. The following are its generic characters, as given by Professor Jamieson, in his Lectures on Natural History, in the University of Edinburgh.

Front Teeth. Six both above and below; the two lateral ones of the lower-jaw longer than the rest, and lobed, with small or secondary teeth at their internal base.

Canine teeth, - - - solitary.

Grinders, five or six on each side, the first approximated to the canine teeth.

Tongue - - - - smooth.

Snout - - - - prominent.

Eyes furnished with a militating membrane.

The hair is of a great length, and the limbs are of an enormous size, and of a very unseemly shape. I have tasted the flesh of the one we killed, and think it by no means bad eating; it had, however, rather a fishy taste. The paw, when dried and smoked, is considered a delicious morsel. Among the Chinese the flesh is considered as one of the greatest rarities, insomuch, that, as Du Halde informs us, the emperor will send fifty or a hundred leagues into Tartary to procure them for a great entertainment. At the approach of winter they become extremely fat; a hundred pounds have been taken from a single beast at this time of the year. Their skins are used for a variety of purposes. By the Esquimeaux they are used for the purpose of making boots, shoes, and other articles of dress. In this country they are sold principally for covers of coach-boxes. The length of the one, whose history I have related, measured thirteen feet. The tendons, when split, are used by the Esquimeaux as a substitute for thread; for which purpose, if we might judge by the neatness of their workmanship, it answers admirably. They appear to be confined to the coldest parts of our globe, being found as far north as any navigators have yet been able to penetrate.

July the 28th, we continued to force our way through the ice; weather uncommonly fine; atmosphere quite clear, and of a pure azure tint.

July 29th. This day, about two o'clock P. M., we first got sight of Upper Savage Island, situated in N. lat. 62°. 25'. W. long. 70'.

This island is about two miles in circumference, and consists merely of a vast lofty perpendicular rock, rising like a cone, in an easy ascent from the sea. It had not the least appearance of verdure, or vegetation of any kind.

On the back part of this island we met with a large commodious harbour, surrounded in part by vast mountains and numerous fields of ice. We expected to get a passage in this direction; but, after tacking about between land and ice the entire night, we were obliged to give up the attempt.

This is the bay to which Captain Wales, in his interesting account of these regions, alludes: "It may," he says, "be worthy of remark, that the island of God's Mercies; or, as some call it, Upper Savage Island, lies in the mouth of an inlet running northward, out of which come the greater part of those islands of ice which are so much taken notice of in these parts."

I have been told by gentlemen in the Hudson's Bay Company's service, that some of their ships have formerly been driven by the ice into this inlet, where they found a fine open sea, without any bounds, that they could see, to the northward. This inlet, Captain Wales calls the North Bay.

July 31st. The weather continues remarkably fine and clear; thermometer in the shade 49°. Moored alongside a field of ice.

August 1st. This day, about ten o'clock A. M., we got sight of the north shore, distant about ten leagues. The whole of this coast exhibited a very barren appearance; the mountains rising suddenly out of the sea, and being composed of rocks, which are thinly covered with black peat earth.

Several fires were kindled along the shore, for the purpose, we presumed, of giving us notice that the natives intended visiting us. Our conjectures we soon found to be true, for, about four o'clock in the afternoon, word was brought down to the cabin that the Esquimeaux Indians were in sight. This being an event long and anxiously wished for, we all hastened on deck immediately. They were not more than thirty yards from the ship. The ice being very thick, they were obliged to carry their canoes and articles for traffic almost the entire way. When they had got within a short distance of the vessel, they all set up a loud cry, every one repeating the word chimò, chimò,* which, in their language, signifies trade. They had no sooner got along-side than they began to traffic. The articles which they offered for sale were—whalebone, bags of blubber, with half-frozen, half-putrid flesh; skins of different animals, as of the bear, rabbit, hare, seal, and deer; dried salmon, dogs, a few fresh fowls; toys of various kinds, as models of their canoes, dresses, &c.

In return they got glass beads, old knives, hatchets, buttons, pins, and needles; gimblets, scissars, pieces of old iron-hoops, which *they prized very highly;* brass-rings, tin-pots, kettles, saws, files, &c.

It would be difficult to give expression to the feelings of gratification, delight, and surprise, which, in hurried succession, passed through my mind on first getting a view of these untutored savages; their manners, persons, dress, language, every thing, in short, so completely different from what

---

* The word chimò is also made use of as a term of friendship.

we are accustomed to in civilized life, that one would almost fancy them the natives of a different planet altogether.

In stature the Esquimeaux is inferior to the generality of Europeans. I have never seen any of them exceed five feet in height, excepting one, who was five feet four inches. Their faces are broad, and approach more to the rounded form than that of the European; their cheek-bones are high; their cheeks round and plump, mouth large, and lips slightly everted; the glabella, or interval between the eyes, is flat and very broad; the nose is small, but not flat, as some writers have described; their eyes, in general, are of a deep black; some, however, are of a dark chesnut-colour; they appear very small, owing to the eye-lids being so much encumbered with fat; the head is large; hair uniformly long, lank, and of a black colour; their eye-lids appeared tender, owing, I suppose, to the piercing winds and strong glare of light reflected from the snow in winter-time; the ears are situated far back on the head, and are moveable; their bodies are large, square, and robust, chest high, shoulders very broad; their hands and feet remarkably small;* there is, however, no sudden diminution; both extremities appear to taper from above, downwards in a wedge-like shape. Their boots and shoes being made of undressed leather, being also very clumsy, I did not for some time take particular notice of their feet. I happened, however, to observe one of the men on the quarter-deck endeavouring to draw on a pair of boots, which he had just purchased from the man whose measurement I have given; the leg passed on easy enough until it came to the lower part, when it was suddenly arrested, nor could he force it further, though he tugged and pulled at it for a considerable time. They are of a deep tawney, or rather copper-coloured complexion. The assertion that they have got no beard must be treated as an idle tale; the fact is, it no sooner appears than, from motives of comfort, and, perhaps, of cleanliness, they pluck it out by the root, having no more convenient way of removing it. I recollect bringing one of the young men, whose beard was just beginning to make its appearance, down to the cabin, and showing him the mode of using a razor: the poor fellow appeared highly delighted; he placed himself before a glass, and really imitated the process of shaving very well; however, he nicked himself in two or three places, at which he laughed very heartily. I did not remark that difference of voice in the young and adult, which

---

* Small hands and feet they possess in common with the Chinese, Kamschatkans, New Hollanders, Peruvians, and Hottentots.

is so very remarkable in these countries; males and females, young and old, had all the same low, husky, whispering kind of voice.*

I shall here give a few words of their language, which I occasionally wrote down during their visits to us.

Whalebone	Sukok.
What's this	Oomena.
A knife	Mukmamuk.
Water	Emik.
Give us	Pelite.
Women	Challeneer.
Blubber	Tuktoo.
A paddle	Poatik.
Go off	Twa wi.
A saw	Kutaswabbo.
An arrow	Katso.
A bow	Petiksik.
A canoe	Porta vinigar.
A boat	Kájak.
A dog	Miké.
Hair	Nootshad.
The foot	Itikak.
An egg	Minniguk.

* This hoarse, whispering kind of voice was very observable in the young Esquimeaux who was at Edinburgh last year; though he had been, when I saw him, near eight months in the country, he still spoke, in ordinary conversation, as if he were whispering. He was a very fine young man, aged about nineteen, and had been a widower for a considerable time. It was surprising to see how soon he adopted the European customs: when shewn into a room, he bowed very gracefully, and was very mild and tractable in his manners. This poor fellow had been drifted out to sea in his canoe near a hundred miles, when he fortunately met with one of the homeward-bound Greenland ships, which took him up. I saw him exhibit several times while he remained at Leith; one day, in particular, the whole population of the country appeared assembled for the purpose of witnessing this interesting sight. The shore for a considerable distance, the shrouds of every vessel, the tops of all the houses, were actually swarming with people. He was this day to row in his canoe against a twelve-oared galley. At a given signal they started: in a few seconds, however, though the brawny Scotchmen rowed with all their might, the Esquimeaux was several yards before them. After getting on a considerable distance, having made all things tight, he capsised himself in his canoe, and appeared at the opposite side. He then waited until his almost exhausted competitors came up to him, and again flew along with the swiftness of an arrow. In this way he went on for near two hours. At the close of the contest a subscription, to a very large amount, was made for him, with which the captain purchased several articles of wearing apparel, as also a number of hatchets, saws, tin-pots, &c. to bring over with him as presents to his countrymen.

The eye - - - -   Killik.
A tooth - - - -   Ukak.
One - - - -   Kombuk.
Two - - - -   Tigal.
Three - - - -   Ke.
Rum (this word properly signifies *mad water*) Killaluk.
The head - - -   Niakok.
The moon - - -   Takok.
A rein-deer - - -   Tuktoo.
A woman's boat - -   Oomiak.

The dresses of this singular people are very curious; and, considering the rude instruments with which they are manufactured, of uncommon neatness. They are made of the skins of the rein-deer, seals, and birds. The outer garment resembles somewhat a waggoner's smock-frock; it is not, however, so long or so loose; it is sewed up in the front as high as the chin. To the top part a cap or hood is fastened, resembling very much the head of the cloaks now so much used in these countries; in cold or wet weather they draw this over their heads, and by means of a running string, they can make it lie as close to the face as they choose. The women's jackets differ somewhat from those of the men; the hood is much larger, and the bottom, instead of being cut even round like the men's, slopes off from the thigh downwards, forming, both behind and before, a long flap, the pointed extremity of which reaches below the knees. Many of the women had a train to their jackets sufficiently long to reach to their heels. The women's jackets also differ from those of the men in being more profusely ornamented with stripes of different coloured skins, which are inserted in a very neat and tasty manner. This outer garment is most usually made of seal-skins; some of them, however, are made of deer-skins; others of bird's-skins, neatly sewed together. A few of them, I observed, wore under their outer-jacket a kind of garment not unlike a shirt, and consisting of a number of seal's bladders sewed together. Their breeches are formed either of seal-skin or of the thin-haired skins of the rein-deer; they are gathered at top like a purse, and tied round their waists. Their boots and shoes are formed of the same materials, and are soled with the skin of the sea-horse. The men's boots are drawn tight about their knees by means of a running-string; their shoes are made to tie in close to the ankle by the same contrivance. The women's boots are made to come up as high as the hips; they are at this part very wide, and made to stand off by means of a strong bow of whalebone passed round the top. Into these they put the children when tired with carrying them on

ESQUIMAUX SPECTACLES.

Pub. for, M. Brand.

their backs. In place of thread they make use of the sinews of the rein-deer, the fibres of which they split very fine, and afterwards twist them in double or triple plies, according as they are,required. Their needles are made either of ivory, or of the very fine bones of birds and fishes. A few of them, however, have got steel needles.

For the purpose of guarding off the intense light reflected from the snow, they make use of a very ingenious kind of spectacles, or snow-eyes, as they call them. They are formed from one solid piece of wood, and are excavated on the inside for the purpose of receiving the bridge of the nose and projecting part of the eye-ball. Opposite to either eye is a narrow transverse slit, about an inch and a half long. In front they are sloped off on either side at an oblique angle. At top there is a small horizontal ledge, which projects out for about an inch. They are tied behind by means of a slip of seal-skin, which is attached to either extremity of the wood.* The one that I have got in my possession measures about four inches in length and two in breadth. Mr. Ellis asserts, that when they would observe any object at a great distance, they commonly look through them as we do through a telescope.

Their canoes are deserving of particular attention, as well from the peculiarity of their form as for their neatness, and even elegance with which they are constructed. They are in general about twenty feet long, two feet broad at the widest part, and of an oblong shape. The frame-work is made of pieces of wood or whalebone, fastened together by means of the sinews of animals; they are covered with seal-skin parchment all over, with the exception of a central aperture, which is left large enough to admit the body of a man; into this the Esquimeaux thrusts himself up to the waist, his feet being stretched forward. To the central opening a flat hoop is fitted, rising about a couple of inches; to this a skin is attached, which he fastens so tight about him as to exclude all wet; the rim also serves the purpose of preventing any water, which may have lodged on the deck, from getting into the canoe. The paddle of the Equimeaux is about ten feet long; narrow in the centre; broad and flat at either extremity: when seated in his canoe

---

* De Paw gives the following description of this curious contrivance— " Le danger d'être aveuglés par la neige, a encore enseigné aux Eskimaux à se servir d'une espece de lunettes qu'ils portent tout l'été sur les yeux, ces sont deux planches minces, percées en deux endroits avec une alêne ou une arrête de poisson de sorte qu'il n'y a qu'une très-petite ouverture pour le passage de la lumiere; cet instrument qu'on attache derriere la tête avec un boyau de phocas, &c.—*Vid. De Paw sur les Americans.*

he takes hold of it by the centre, dips either end in the water alternately, and thus he moves with incredible celerity; so great, indeed, that an English boat, with twelve oars, is not able to keep up with him.* The broad flat part is generally inlaid, in a very tasty and fanciful manner, with portions of sea-horse teeth, cut into a variety of forms.

The dexterity with which they manage these canoes is really astonishing. No weather can prevent them from going out to sea; they venture out in the midst of tempestuous whirlwinds, and driving snows, with as much composure as if it were a perfect calm. Even though the sea should break over them, in an instant they are again seen flying along the ridge of the wave.

But what appears still more extraordinary, is the power they possess of completely upsetting themselves in their canoes, so as to hang perpendicularly under the water. I shall relate an instance of this. Captain Turner was one day standing on the quarter-deck while the Indians were along-side trading; he observed at some distance an Esquimeaux paddling up and down, as if for amusement: having made a sign to him to come over, he told him he would give him a knife and a few needles, in case he would capsise himself in his canoe. The Indian immediately made tight all his running-strings, lapped some skins about his body, and having thus secured himself from the water entering, he looked at Captain Turner with a very significant air; he then inclined his body towards the surface of the water, and instantly dipped down; here he remained suspended for a few seconds, when he appeared at the opposite side in his former upright position. This he did three successive times. When he had done, he shook himself, laughed very heartily, and, after getting his knife and needles, paddled off.

The value which they set on their canoes is, as we might naturally, suppose, very great; indeed, they will very rarely part with them, unless they get in exchange a considerable number of valuable articles, such as a tin-pot, a kettle, a saw, and perhaps a few gimblets. Captain Turner purchased one of the neatest I think I have ever seen: it was quite new, and was very beautifully ornamented. The hoop which surrounds the central aperture, instead of wood, was made of highly-polished ivory. The workmanship on the extremity of the paddle was exquisite. Before the owner parted with it he paddled up to an elderly man at some distance, whom, the captain told us,

---

* See page 29.

was his father; which, indeed, we had conjectured, as well from his aged appearance as from the great respect this young man appeared to pay to him. After deliberating for some time he returned, and told Mr. Turner he should have the canoe, and immediately set about emptying it of its contents. The articles which he took out he put into his father's; and having given it up to the captain, he stretched himself quite flat behind his parent, covering his face with his hands ; here he lay quite composed, without the smallest motion. The father having received his tin-pot, kettle, hatchet, and a couple of files, rowed off. The day following we heard that this poor fellow had slipped off from behind his father while on their way to shore, and was drowned.

The avidity of these poor people for traffic, exceeded any thing I could have had an idea of. Many of them, after parting with all their goods, stripped themselves almost naked, and began to dispose of their clothes for the merest trifles. One man gave a very beautiful seal-skin jacket for an old rusty knife. Another parted with his breeches and boots for a file and a few needles. Another with a complete suit of clothes for a saw and a few pieces of old iron. At length, thinking they had exhausted our entire stock of hardware, they began to barter with the ship's crew for their old clothes. It frequently afforded us a humorous sight to see those poor creatures disposing of their whole and comfortable, though rudely-formed garments, for a seaman's old working-jacket, or perhaps for an old checked shirt, through the numerous rents and apertures of which their copper-coloured skins here and there made its appearance. They generally paddled away in a great hurry, after completing the bargain, fearing lest the purchaser might possibly repent; an apprehension which I could assure them was quite groundless. One of them purchased an old red night-cap from the cook, and having adjusted it on his head, he looked at himself in a glass, and laughed most immoderately.

Several of them had bags of blubber, mixed with half-putrid half-frozen flesh ; these they offered for sale with great eagerness, and appeared very much surprised that they got no purchasers. Being anxious to examine their contents, I was induced to buy one ; on opening it, however, such a shocking stench proceeded from it, that I very cheerfully restored it to the original possessor. I had no sooner returned it to him, than applying the open extremity to his mouth, took a drink from it, licked his lips, and laid it aside very carefully. Others had raw seal's-flesh, which they also seemed to consider a great luxury. I have frequently seen them take out a piece, eat a portion of it, and, when done, lick their fingers and lips, as if they had been feeding on the fragments of some sumptuous banquet.

In consequence of the great number of canoes that were alongside the ship (no less than forty), they frequently tilted against each other; when this happened, they did not appear at all irritated, but rowed aside with the greatest good-humour. A few of them made off without giving any thing in return for the articles they had got from us ; the rest did not appear to notice it, nor did they at all interfere.* After paddling away a few yards from the ship, they generally turned about and laughed very heartily at those whom they had thus tricked. When disappointed in any article which they expected to get, they appeared very much irritated.

I recollect seeing on the canoe of one of the men an apparently very nice skin ; I immediately held up a file to the Indian, and then pointed to the skin, thus intimating that I wished to exchange with him. On close examination, however, I found that it was completely rotten, and all over in holes, and signified to him that I did not think it sufficient value for the file. He immediately took up his paddle, and winding it round his head, made a desperate blow at me, the full benefit of which I should have received, but for the celerity with which I made up the gang-way.

Several of the men had bows and arrows ; they could not, however, be induced to part with them, owing, as the captain supposed, to their being then at war with some neighbouring tribe of Indians.

During the first day, we were not visited by any of the women ; the following morning, however, about ten o'clock, a large boatful came alongside, and in about an hour afterwards several others. The women's boat, or umiak, as they term it, differs very much in form from that of the men, being entirely open at top, and so large as to be capable of carrying thirty or forty persons. They are made of the same materials as those of the men. In the first boat that arrived there were about twenty women, and the same number of children. At the stern of it I observed an aged infirm old woman, with a thoughtful melancholy countenance ; there was also something wild and unsettled in her looks. A highly-polished plate of brass surrounded her forehead, somewhat like a coronet ; her hair was collected into small bobs, by means of the sinews of animals, and from each was suspended the tooth

---

* This, however, arose a good deal, I fancy, from their companions being so much occupied in trading.

of some land-animal. In other respects her dress wss like that of the rest: she appeared to have the command of the entire, as none of them bartered, even the most trifling artiele, without first asking her permission. I uniformly observed that men and women, when they had gotten any thing in exchange, immediately commenced licking it, to intimate, as I afterwards learned, that it was then their property. While trading with the women, I had an opportunity of observing how far they were from despising all sort of authority; they all appeared attentive to the voice of wisdom, which time and experience had conferred on the aged. It is age which teaches experience, and experience is the only source of knowledge amongst a barbarous people. I remarked that several of the mothers pointed repeatedly to the children's heads, as I supposed for the purpose of selling them; in this, however, I was quite mistaken, as they have for their children the greatest affection, and do not part with them for any consideration. I understood afterwards, that it was merely to recommend them to my notice, in order that I might give them something. The children, most of whom were about nine or ten years old, appeared of very lively dispositions, and many of them were really very well looking. I did not observe that they reprimanded them in any way; indeed, I am told that this is never done. Liberty is their darling passion; it is this which makes life supportable, and to it they are ready to sacrifice every thing; their education is directed, therefore, in such a manner as to cherish this disposition to the utmost. Reason, they say, will guide their children when they come to the use of it, and before that time their faults cannot be very considerable; but blows, by producing a slavish motive to action, might damp their free and martial spirit.

A few of the women had young children at the breast. I recollect one in particular, who, while very busy trading, was much annoyed with the crying of her young squaw, about six months old, which she had in the hood of her garment. Unwilling to be at the trouble of holding it to the breast,* she went up to the stern of the boat, where the old woman was sitting, and took out a small bag of blubber, applied the open extremity to the infant's mouth, and pressing it between her thumb and forefinger, she in this way forced a quantity of it into the young thing's mouth; the crying immediately ceased, and, in a few minutes, the young savage was fast asleep.

---

* I may here remark, that their breasts, though very long and flaccid, are by no means of sufficient length to throw over their shoulders, as some have asserted.

When the women had disposed of their merchandise, they all cried out, " Twa wi, twa wi;" and then pointed to the ship, thus intimating their wish that we should leave them.

In the evening about sixty of them, men, women, and children, came on board. The women appeared highly delighted with the dancing, and imitated it very closely. We shewed three or four of the men the two bears we had taken on the ice. They appeared very much terrified at the sight of them, and uttered something which I could not understand. One of them pointed to his side, where I observed a very large scar ; he then made a growling kind of noise, and ran away with great speed. I thence concluded that this poor fellow had been bit by a bear some time previous. Tea being announced, we brought several of them down to the cabin, and placed before them wine, rum, sugar, bread, milk, and a variety of other things; but they rejected them all with the greatest disgust; sugar they appeared to dislike particularly. Every one of them, I observed, spit it out, and cleansed their mouths after it.

We happened to have for dinner that day some very nice roasted pork, and being anxious to see if they would eat of it, I placed a large slice on a plate before one of them ; I also laid a knife and fork before him. He appeared to like the meat well enough, but his knife and fork he managed very badly ; for instead of introducing the piece on the fork into his mouth, the point of it went off to his cheek, while the hand went to his mouth. I was much amused with this singular instance of the strong force of habit. The children behaved themselves remarkably well. We could not, however, prevail on them to sit more than a few minutes in one position. When placed in a chair, they would look down on either side of it, jump up, and run about the cabin. Being anxious to hear what the mother would say in case I attempted chastising one of them, I began to pull the ears of a very fine boy, about twelve years old, who was sitting beside me. The mother immediately stood up, and gave me a very fierce angry look. Observing that she was much displeased, I immediately began to pat him on the head, and gave him a few beads. She instantly recovered her good-humour, and cried out, " Chimo, chimo." There was only one of them attempted to pilfer. Happening to look round rather suddenly, I observed one of them slipping a silver spoon into his boot. I immediately arrested his hand, took the spoon, and shewed it to his companions. He did not appear at all ashamed of being detected, but laughed very heartily.

A MOONLIGHT SCENE ON THE ICE.

About ten o'clock they left us; the greater part of them made towards the shore, to which they were directed by the placid light of a full unclouded moon. We gazed after them for a considerable time, until at length they were lost in the dark and shadowy line of land which lay before us. Those who remained about the ship, slept on the ice the entire night, with merely the interposition of a few seal-skins. Before retiring to rest, I observed them take from their canoes some raw seal's-flesh and bags of blubber, on which they appeared to feast very sumptuously.

I remarked, that one of them kept watch in turn during the entire night; he walked about on the ice with a harpoon in his hand. This I fancy was more from a dread of being attacked by the bears, than from any apprehension they had of being attacked by the Europeans. A few of us remained on deck until a very late hour; at one time watching every motion of our northern friends, at another, gazing with astonishment and delight on the brilliant and impressive scenery with which we were surrounded. While thinking on the miserable condition of the squallid inhabitants of this dreary inhospitable climate, I was forcibly reminded of the following beautiful lines of Cowper:—

> ————" Within the enclosure of your rocks
> Nor herds have ye to boast, nor bleating flocks;
> No fertilizing streams your fields divide,
> That show, revers'd, the villas on their side:
> No groves have ye; no cheerful sound of bird,
> Or voice of turtle, in your land is heard;
> No grateful eglantine regales the smell
> Of those that walk at evening, where you dwell."

With regard to the diseases to which these poor savages are subject, I must be very brief. From personal observation I learned but little, and from enquiry still less. I may here remark, that I did not observe any appearance whatever of small-pox among them; neither had the children or parents any marks or deformity of any kind. Indeed, it is said, that they put to death those children that are born hunch-backed, blind, or defective in any limb; and, in proof of this, it is advanced, that when they have been formed into societies, and that the vigilance of their rulers prevents such murders, the number of the deformed is greater than in any country in Europe. I may remark, however, that this account is denied by very respectable authorities. The only diseases which fell under my observation, if diseases they could well be called, were the affection of the eye-lids, of which I have already spoken; epistaxis, or bleeding from the nose, and hypochondriaris; the

former of these arising probably from the large quantity of
animal food which they consume, and from their being so
constantly in a stooping posture : it did not appear to give
them the smallest uneasiness. I have seen the blood trickle
down very copiously, without their even appearing to notice
it ; they allowed it quietly to trickle into the mouth, and when
it took an irregular course down by the angle of the mouth,
they wiped it away with the cuff of their jacket. Hypochondriaris is a very frequent complaint among them, induced,
probably, by the physical circumstances of their situation, and
the long confinement which they are compelled to submit to
during their long and dreary winter; yet their general tem-
perament does not appear to be a melancholic one. I have
often been struck most forcibly with the vivacity of their disposition, when contrasted with the wretchedness which their
external condition displayed. The women are said to bear
but few children. I shall conclude these few remarks, by
observing, that springs being very rare in their country, the
water which they use is principally supplied by melted snow;
nevertheless, I have not observed any of those glandular
swellings which so frequently occur in the Alpine regions of
Europe and Asia.

That the Esquimeaux Indians were originally Greenland-
ers is, I believe, now generally admitted. Indeed, the simi-
larity of their dress, canoes, paddles, language, &c. must, I
conceive, remove every shadow of doubt on the subject.
They principally inhabit the sea-coast, as well for the purpose
of being convenient to the sea, as that they may avoid the
North-American Indians, there having long subsisted between
those two tribes a deadly and implacable hatred. Whenever
they come to an engagement, the North-American Indian,
being better armed, and of a more muscular frame, is sure to
come off victorious. It generally terminates with the mas-
sacre of the entire party, men, women, and children. Mr.
Hearne, in his interesting voyage to Coppermine River, giving
an account of one of those savage scenes which he had witnessed, relates the following very affecting circumstance : —
" My horror," remarks Mr. Hearne, " was much increased, at
seeing a young girl, seemingly about eighteen years of age,
killed so near me, that when the first spear was stuck into her
side, she fell down at my feet, and twisted round my legs, so
that it was with difficulty I could disengage myself from her
dying grasp. As two Indian men pursued this unfortunate
victim, I solicited very hard for her life; but the murderers
made no reply till they had stuck both their spears through
her body, and transfixed her to the ground. They then looked

me sternly in the face, and began to ridicule me, by asking
if I wanted an Esquimeaux wife? and paid not the smallest
regard to the shrieks and agony of the poor wretch who was
twining round their spears like an eel! Indeed, after receiving much abusive language from them on the occasion, I was
at length obliged to desire that they would be more expedi-
tious in dispatching their victim out of her misery, otherwise I
should be obliged, out of pity, to assist in the friendly office of
putting an end to the existence of a fellow-creature who was
so cruelly wounded. On this request being made, one of the
Indians hastily drew his spear from the place where it was
first lodged, and pierced it through her breast near the heart.
The love of life, however, even in this most miserable state,
was so predominant, that though this might justly be called
the most merciful act that could be done for the poor creature, it seemed to be unwelcome, for, though much exhausted
by pain and loss of blood, she made several efforts to ward
off the friendly blow. My situation, and the horror of my
mind at beholding this scene of butchery, cannot easily be
conceived, much less described: though I summed up all the
fortitude I was master of on the occasion, it was with difficulty
I could refrain from tears; and I am confident that my features
must have feelingly expressed how sincerely I was affected
at the barbarous scene I then witnessed. Even at this moment I cannot reflect on the transactions of that horrid day
without shedding tears."

Notwithstanding the shocking persecutions to which these
poor creatures are exposed, there are no people in all the vast
variety of climate, of soil, and of civilization, so attached to
the land of their birth; affording a striking proof that this
strong passion is by no means commensurate with the physical advantages of the soil. The contrary, indeed, appears
to be the fact; the wretchedness of their condition, and
dreadful severity of their climate, appearing rather to multiply and strengthen those ties of attachment. The few* who
have been brought or rather forced away to this country,
though treated in the most kind and tender manner, and
provided with every comfort, have still sighed after their
floating mountains, their beloved seals and smoky wigwams.
No distance, however remote, nor lapse of time, however

---

* Les premiers individues de cette nation qu'on ait vus en Europe, y
avoient été améne par le navigateur Forbisher, qui présenta, en 1577, trois
Esquimeaux á la reine Elizabeth : on les promena sur de petits chevaux de
corse, & ils servirent pendant quelque jours d'amusement à la populace, tou-
jours avide de spectacle insensés.—*De Paw sur les Americans,* vol. i. p. 258.

great, appeared capable of eradicating this strong passion from their hearts.*

> But where to find that happiest spot below,
> Who can direct, when all pretend to know?
> The shuddering tenant of the frigid zone
> Boldly proclaims that happy spot his own;
> Extols the treasures of his stormy seas,
> And his long nights of revelry and ease.

With regard to their dispositions, were I to judge from what I had an opportunity of seeing, I should suppose them to be a good-humoured, mild, tractable race of people. Others, however, have represented them in a very different light, accusing them of cruelty, theft, deceit, and, in short, every vice. It is probable, however, that these accounts have been received from the North-American Indians, who, as I already mentioned, have long been their inveterate enemies. Captain Wales, who resided for many years in Hudson's Bay, speaking of them, says, " I have had, whilst at Churchill, an exceedingly good opportunity of learning the dispositions of these people, as several of them come almost every year by their own free-will to reside at the factory, and can with truth aver, that never people less deserved the epithets of ' treacherous, cruel, fawning, and suspicious ;' the contrary of which is remarkably true in every particular. They are open, generous, and unsuspecting; addicted too much, it must be owned, to passion ; and too apt to revenge what they think an injury, if an opportunity offers at the moment, but are almost instantly cool, without requiring any acknowledgment on your part (which they account shameful), and, I verily believe, never remember the circumstance afterwards. Mr. Ellis observes," continues Captain Wales, " that they are apt to pilfer from strangers, easily encouraged to a degree of boldness, but as easily frightened." Now, I cannot help thinking, that he would have conveyed a much better idea of them if he had expressed himself thus : They are bold and enterprising, even to enthusiasm, whilst there is a probability of success crowning their endeavours ; but wise enough to desist, when inevitable destruction stares them in the face.

---

* They are extremely, I might say obstinately, attached to their own customs and manner of living. Some of them, who were taken prisoners by the southern Indians, when they were boys, and brought to the factories, and there kept several years, have still regretted their absence from their native country. One of these, after having been fed on English diet, being present when one of the Englishmen was cutting up a seal, from whence the train-oil ran very plentifully, licked up what he could save with his hands, and said, " Ah! commend me to my own dear country, where I could get my belly full of this."—*Ellis's Voyage to Hudson's Bay,* p. 63.

Of their religious opinions I have been able to learn but little. Our imperfect acquaintance with their language; their avidity for traffic, which was so great as to prevent their attending to any enquiries on such matters; these, together with the shortness of our stay among them, rendered it very difficult to ascertain any thing of a satisfactory nature on that subject. Some have very foolishly supposed that they adored a small figure resembling a bear, and made from the tooth of the sea-horse: it is, however, merely intended as a kind of amusement during their long and tedious winter-evenings. From the body, which is perforated with a number of small holes, hangs a slender piece of stick, pointed; and, on this, they endeavour to catch the bear, just in the same way as the cup and ball is used by the boys of this country.

The following conversation, which is related by the accurate historian Crantz, to have passed between a converted Greenlander and one of the Moravian missionaries, will probably afford a better idea of their religious sentiments than any account I could give. The missionary having expressed his wonder how they could formerly lead such a senseless life, void of all reflection, one of them answered as follows: " It is true we were ignorant heathens, and knew nothing of a God or a Saviour; and, indeed, who should tell us of him, till you came?—But thou must not imagine, that no Greenlander thinks about these things. I, myself, have often thought a kajak (boat), with all its tackle and implements, does not grow into existence of itself; but must be made by the labour and ingenuity of man, and one that does not understand it would directly spoil it. Now, the meanest bird has far more skill displayed in its structure than the best kajak, and no man can make a bird. But there is a still far greater art shown in the formation of a man than of any other creature. Who was it that made him? I bethought me, he proceeded from his parents, and they from their parents. But some must have been the first parents: whence did they come? Common report informs me they grew out of the earth. But if so, why does it not still happen that men grow out of the earth? And from whence did this same earth itself, the sea, the sun, the moon, and stars, rise into existence? Certainly there must be some Being who made all these things—a Being that always was, and can never cease to be. He must be inexpressibly more mighty, knowing, and wise, than the wisest man. He must be very good too; because, every thing that he has made is good, useful, and necessary for us. Ah! did I but know him, how would I love him and honour him! But who has seen him? Who has conversed with him?—none of us poor men.

Yet there may be men too that know something of him. Oh! could I but speak with such! Therefore, (said he) as soon as ever I heard you speak of this Great Being, I believed it directly with all my heart, because I had so long desired it." They all believe in a future state, but differ very much with regard to its nature and situation. In general, they imagine it to be a better state than this temporal life, and that it will never end. As they procure the greater part of their food from the bosom of the sea, therefore many of them place their Elysium in the abysses of the ocean, or bowels of the earth, and think the deep cavities of the rocks are the avenues leading to it. There, they imagine, dwells a Tonjarink and his mother; there a joyous summer is perpetual, and a shining sun obscured by no night; there is the fair limpid stream, and an exuberance of fowls, fishes, and their beloved seals, and these are all to be caught without toil; nay, they are even found in a great kettle ready drest. But to these places none must approach, except those that have been dextrous and diligent at their work; that have performed great exploits, have mastered many whales and seals, have undergone great hardships, have been drowned in the sea, or died in childbed.

In reviewing the manners of these untutored Indians, some few particulars excepted, we are presented with an interesting view of primeval happiness, arising chiefly from the fewness of their wants, and their universal equality. The latter destroys all distinction among them, except those of age and personal merit, and promotes the ease, harmony, and freedom of their mutual conversation and intercourse. This facilitates the happiness of the Indian lover, who finds no obstacles to the fruition of his desires, from inequality of rank or fortune, or from the views which ambition or envy inspire; and this annihilates all envy and discontent. But the advantages resulting from the paucity and simplicity of their desires, contribute to their felicity in a more eminent degree. Those who have been unhappily familiarised to all the various refinements of luxury and effeminacy which attend the great, and whose deluded imaginations esteem them essential to happiness, will hardly believe, that an Indian, without any other covering but what an undressed seal-skin affords, with a shelter which cannot deserve the name of a house, and a few culinary and domestic utensils, could form any pretensions to happiness; and yet, if I may be allowed to judge from external appearances, the happiness of these people may justly be envied, even by the wealthy of the most refined countries; as their happy ignorance of those extravagant desires and endless pursuits which agitate the great luxurious world, excludes every wish beyond their present enjoyment. The fewness and simplicity of their wants, with the abundance of means for their supply, and the ease with which they are acquired, renders all division of property useless. Each amicably participates the ample blessings of an extensive country, without rivalling his neighbour or interrupting his happiness. This renders all government and all laws unnecessary, as in such a state there can be no temptations to dishonesty, fraud, injustice, or violence; nor, indeed, any desires which may not be gratified with innocence.

To acquire the art of dispensing with all imaginary wants, and contenting ourselves with the real conveniences of life, is one of the noblest exertions of reason, and a most useful acquisition, as it elevates the mind above the vicissitudes of fortune. Socrates justly observes, that those who want least, approach nearest to the gods, who want nothing. The simplicity, however, which is so apparent in the manners of the Indians is not the effect of a philosophical self-denial, but of the ignorance of more refined enjoyments, which, however, produces effects equally happy with those which result from the most austere philosophy; and their manners present an emblem of the fabled Elysian fields, where individuals need not the assistance of each other, but yet preserve a constant intercourse of love and friendship.

Several modern philosophers, as Rousseau, Lord Monboddo, and others, from observing the innocence and happiness which savage nations enjoy, though ignorant of the liberal arts, have from thence inferred, that arts and sciences were prejudicial to civilized society. In this, however, they are egregiously mistaken. The ills of civilized society have their source in the unnatural and unequal distribution of property, which is necessarily produced by the different degrees of sagacity, industry, and frugality in individuals, transmitted to, and augmented by an accumulating posterity, till the disproportion in the possessions of different individuals becomes enormous, and creates a thousand unnatural distinctions among mankind, enabling some to squander the bread of thousands in a profusion of satiating pleasures, while multitudes are suffering from want, insulted by every species of subordinate tyranny. Thus the excessive disproportion of wealth renders the poor miserable, without augmenting the happiness of the rich. When this disparity becomes considerable, then, and not till then, luxury advances with all its attendant pleasures and refinements; which, without communicating an increase of happiness to those who enjoy them, tempt those who have them not to endeavour to acquire them by unjust and violent means.

Mankind are then taught to connect the idea of happiness with those of dress, equipage, affluence, and all the various amusements which luxury has invented; thence they become slaves to a thousand imaginary wants, which become the source of envy, discontent, fraud, injustice, perjury, and violence. Thus man becomes the author of moral evil.

To conclude I may remark, that every kind of life has its peculiar advantages as well as evils. The vices of civilized countries, though more numerous are less terrible. Artificial wants extend the circle of our pleasures; luxury in the rich, promotes industry and the arts, and feeds and clothes the labouring poor, who would otherwise starve; thus we derive advantage not only from the follies but the vices of each other. Whether, therefore, we pass our life in the rustic simplicity and ignorance of an Esquimeaux Indian, or in the endless pleasures of refinements and luxury, we shall arrive at the same end, and, perhaps, with an equal portion of happiness, as far, at least, as it depends on external enjoyments, abstracting only the miseries of real want and disease. However various the conditions of mankind may be, the distribution of happiness and misery in life is far from being so unequal as is generally believed; good and evil are indiscriminately mingled in the Cup of Being : the monarch in his purple, and the beggar in his rags, are exposed to their respective cares and afflictions. Agreeable objects, by possession and familiarity, lose their aptitude and capacity for pleasing, and, in every state of life, hope ends in disappointment, and enjoyment in satiety.

August 4th. The ice beginning to loose for a considerable distance around the ship, we took in our anchors and made sail; during this day we got several very severe knocks from the ice, in consequence of which we were obliged to keep the pumps going day and night.

On the 6th we were again visited by the Esquimeaux. Many of the women had their faces tattooed in a very curious manner; one of them, whose entire face was almost completely covered with these marks, had her hair collected into large bobs, from which hung several bears-claws. Their principal articles of traffic consisted of dogs, whalebone, and bones of the sea-horse dried, and of a beautiful white colour; a few had small bags, containing mosses, lichens, and a few other cryptogamous plants.

The dogs were for the most part white; some, however, were spotted, and others of a black colour. Their ears are short and erect, and the whole body is covered with long hair; their legs and feet resemble very much those of the bear. They do not bark, but make a growling kind of noise. Sometimes they are eaten by the natives; when the skins are used as coverlets for cloathing, or for bordering and seaming their habits. They are principally used, however, both in this country and in Kamstschatka, for the purpose of drawing their sledges over the frozen snow during the winter-season. Four, five, or six, as circumstances may require, are commonly yoked to the same sledge, and will readily carry these persons with their baggage a journey of fifty English miles a-day.

On the 8th we got in sight of Cape Diggs, lat., as observed, 63° 4′, long. 78° 50′. And on the day following Cape Walsingham came in view, bearing S. W., and in lat. 62° 39′, long. 77° 48′.

August 10th. Finding it impossible to make further progress through the ice, we made fast to an island of prodigious height and extent, and of a very singular shape. The fore part, or that to which we anchored, was hollowed-out in a semicircular form, and was of sufficient extent to afford shelter to the three ships. The back part presented a perpendicular cliff, which could not be less than 300 feet high; the top part presented a surface of about two miles in circumference; in one part raised into rugged fantastic hills, in another depressed into abrupt precipitous vallies. Altogether, this island formed one of the grandest piles I had ever witnessed. About six o'clock a party of us agreed to go on shore. We brought with us a very fine lad, a sailor-boy, who played the German-flute inimitably well, and who had been on this, as well as many other occasions, a very agreeable source of amusement to us. After labouring very hard for near two hours, we at length gained the summit of the island, which we took possession of in the name of his Britannic majesty. Having laid aside our ice-anchors, axes, staffs, &c. we sat down to a collation of bread and cheese, after which we had some wine. At length the lad began playing his flute; the rich and melodious sounds of which being reverberated from the adjacent hills and vallies, gave it an inconceivably grand effect.

The sun still lingered on the verge of the western horizon, appearing, as it were, to rest his " huge disk" on one of the frozen fields of ice. At length, however, after spreading a saffron-coloured suffusion along the huge pile of clouds which now assembled on all sides, like " misfortunes and disasters around a sinking empire and falling monarch," he gently closed the parting day.

> And now they change; a paler shadow strews
> Its mantle o'er the mountains; parting day
> Dies like the dolphin, whom each pang embues

With a new colour as it gasps away,
The last, still loveliest, till—'tis gone—and all is grey.
                              Last Canto of Childe Harold, p. 16.

A night of uncommon fineness succeeded; the moon rose
with unclouded splendour, irradiating with its placid effulgence the surrounding scenery, and giving it, if possible,
a still more interesting appearance. The clearness of the
heavens, the serenity of the air, and the soft tranquillity which
appeared to pervade all nature, contributed to harmonize the
mind, and produce the most calm and pleasing sensations.
On those occasions the soul appears to have an irresistible ten-
dency to rise from the grand and majestic scene to the great
Author of all sublimity.

About eleven o'clock we returned to the vessel, highly gratified with our evening's amusements. Just as we were getting
on board a very melancholy event had nearly happened. The
poor sailor-boy, to whom we were indebted for a great part of
the evening's amusement, unfortunately slipped while getting
up the quarter-deck, and was precipitated into the sea. Ropes
and boat-hooks were instantly got, and in a few minutes we
had the poor fellow safe on board.

On the 12th we made the north-end of Mansell's Island,
situated in lat. 62° 38¼′, long. 80° 33′.

August 15th. Hardly any ice in sight; going about four
knots in the hour; the ship continuing very leaky, we were
obliged to keep the pumps going day and night.

August 20. About half-past one, A. M., the man at the
forecastle shouted out ice a-head. The mate immediately
went up to the bow of the vessel, and found we were running
straight on very heavy ice. Being under a heavy press of
sail, and going at the rate of 7½ knots in the hour, we were
of course much alarmed; fortunately, however, the ship was
readily got about, so that, in a short time, we were completely
clear. After a short tack we again fell in with ice; about
five o'clock, however, A. M., we got into a clear sea. At
nine, A. M., going about 5½ knots in the hour; course S. W.
by W.; wind fair.

On the 21st we got into Hudson's Bay, after which we saw
no more ice. Instead of feasting our eyes with the grand and
impressive scenery which we had so long enjoyed, we had to
encounter three days of almost incessant squalls, sleet, rain,
and a most boisterous sea.

On the 24th it blew a tremendous gale of wind; danger
considerably aggravated by our having made the land too
soon. In a short time the whole horizon was covered with
large foaming billows, which

Swell'd and rag'd and foam'd,
To be exalted with the threat'ning clouds.

In a few minutes all was hurry and confusion; the captain flew himself from one part of the deck to the other with the greatest alertness, to assist, by his own exertions, when fear, or hurry, prevented the sailors from doing their duty. In the middle of this awful scene I was called on to render professional assistance to Mrs. M'Clain, who was seized with labour-pains. It would be difficult to conceive a more unpleasant situation than that in which I was now placed. The dread of being driven on a lee-shore, the howling of the wind among the rigging, the awful sound of the pumps, which we were obliged to keep constantly at work; the cries of my poor patient, who was now suffering the most intense pain which human nature can suffer, all combined with the horribly depressing effects of sea-sickness, contributed to render this the most frightful night I had ever witnessed.

About twelve o'clock, P. M., in consequence of dreadful shouting, I went upon deck, and found every one in the greatest consternation and terror; it appeared we had got in among shoals, and that we had now not more than four-fathom water; in a short time, however, we got into ten-fathom, when we cast two anchors. On these depended all our safety; if they gave way nothing would have saved us from being driven on shore, when we must inevitably have perished; fortunately, however, they held fast. About ten o'clock, A. M., Mrs. M'Clain was, to the great joy of all on board, safely delivered of a daughter. At twelve o'clock the weather began to clear up, and, with the exception of a few showers, was fine all day. A brighter atmosphere now permitted us to get sight of the land, from which we were distant about ten miles. Some grass and twigs were observed floating along-side the ship.

The following morning, while lying in bed, I heard one of the men upon deck say he saw a schooner coming off from the land. We all immediately went upon deck, and found, to our great joy, that this piece of intelligence was correct. In a short time she was along-side. A large quantity of venison was sent us by the governor of York Fort, a present which the reader may readily suppose was most acceptable, as we had hardly tasted any thing for two days.

Wednesday, August 26th, we cast anchor in view of York Fort, lat. 57° 2' N. long. 92° 46'. The day following I went on shore, in company with the rest of the cabin-passengers. The coast, as we approached it, presented a very interesting appearance, being thickly studded with pine, poplar, and juniper, while the tide rippled on in tiny waves towards the white and pebbled beach. After ascending a platform, which projected out for a considerable distance, we were welcomed in a most polite manner by Mr. Ald, the governor. Until you come to the governor's house, nothing is to be seen but a few out-houses, some for storing firs, others for boat-builders. The govornor's house is about 100 yards in breadth, and thirty feet high, consisting of two stories, not unlike an extensive farm-house. Before it, there is a high close railing, for the purpose, I was told, of keeping off the Indians when they get intoxicated, as they are then not only troublesome but dangerous. It is built entirely of wood, cut into square logs, and laid one on top of the other. After partaking of some refreshments, a walk was proposed. As I was most anxious to get a glimpse of the natives, I made towards that part of the shore where I had, on our way up, observed some of their wigwams. Of these I shall now give some account.

The North-American Indians are, for the most part, tall, large boned, and long visaged, with very prominent features. The eye is penetrating, and of a deep black colour. The nose prominent, of an aquiline shape, not at all flattened. The forehead is short and straight. Chin rounded, and projecting slightly. Mouth large, but lips not at all everted. Hair uniformly of a shining black, strait and coarse, having no disposition whatever to curl. On the entire, when viewed in profile, the parts appear more deeply and distinctly marked out than in the Esquimeaux. The ear is not placed so far back on the head, nor is the glabella, or space between the eyes, at all so great as in the last-mentioned tribe. The general expression of countenance is gloomy and severe. Some, however, especially the young men, have a very cheerful animated look. Though the countenance is, generally speaking, such as I have here represented, there is, however, the same variety as we meet with amongst Europeans, contrary to the assertion of some, who have maintained that all the inhabitants of the new world have precisely the same countenance; so that having seen one, you might be said to have seen all. They have but little hair on their chin, or upper lip, owing, as in the case of the Esquimeaux, to its being eradicated immediately on its first appearance. The most unfounded reports have been circulated on this subject, by ignorant, superficial, or prejudiced observers. Some, indeed, have gone so far as to assert that the Americans are destitute of beard altogether, and have represented this as a characteristic peculiarity of this portion of the human race. The concurring testimony, however, of all modern accurate travellers, proves clearly that the Americans have naturally beards, and just as abundant as we find it amongst Europeans : that it is a very general custom with them, as it has been with several Morgolian and Malay tribes, carefully to eradicate this excrescence; but that various tribes, in different parts of the continent, preserve it as other men do.

Gmelin found this practice to exist in Africa : " It is not easy," he says, " to find a Zungoone, nor any man of the neighbouring tribes, with a beard; for they extract the hairs as soon as they appear, and repeat the process until at last no more are formed."

The same circumstance is reported of the Sumatrans, by Marsden ; of the Mindanao islanders, by Forrest; of the Pellew islanders, by Wilson; of the inhabitants of New Guinea, by Cartaret; and of those of Navigators' Isles, by Bougainville. I may add to this evidence, the testimonies of the celebrated navigator Captain Cook; as also that of the most scientific traveller of ancient and modern times, the celebrated Humboldt. Captain Cook, speaking of the inhabitants of Nootka Sound, says, " Some have no beards at all, and others only a thin one on the point of the chin. This does not arise from a deficiency of hair in these parts, but from their plucking it out by the roots; for those who do not destroy it, have not only considerable beards on every part of the chin, but also whiskers, or mustachios, running from the upper lip to the lower jaw, obliquely downwards."

Humboldt, speaking of the South Americans, remarks, " The Mexicans, I have observed, particularly those of the Aztec and Otomite races, have more beard than ever I saw in any other Indians of South America. In the neighbourhood of the capital, almost all the Indians wear mustachios." And again, " I can affirm, that the Indians who inhabit the Torrid Zone of South America have generally some beard ; and that the beard increases when they shave themselves."

The females, or squaws, as they are generally called, differ considerably both in person and features from the men. Instead of being tall, robust, and long-visaged, they are, on the contrary, short, small-boned, with the face approaching more to the rounded form. The colour of the hair is the same in both; the women, however, pay more attention to its being combed smooth behind, so as to flow loose about their shoulders; in front, it is very neatly divided, so as to give a full view of the forehead. They, for the most part, have an expression of mildness and sweetness in their looks. The common dress of the men, in summer, consists of an English blanket thrown loosely round their shoulders; under this a

deer-skin jacket, the sleeves of which are distinct from the
body, so that they can be removed at pleasure. Their small-
clothes and shoes are made of the same materials as the jacket;
the latter, or moccasicus, as they are termed, are generally
embroidered with dyed porcupine's quills, in a very neat and
elegant manner. Some of them wore a coat of scarlet, or
green cloth, made after the military fashion, and ornamented
with a profusion of tin, or silver trinkets, giving them a very
noble and majestic appearance.

The dress of the women differs somewhat from that of the
men : the blanket, instead of being thrown loose about the
shoulders, is brought close round the forehead, somewhat in
form of a hood, and is generally bound round with scarlet, or
green tape ; they also wear a long loose petticoat, made of
some woollen stuff. On Sunday, in place of the blanket, they
wear a piece of green or scarlet cloth, made into the form of
a mantle, and thrown carelessly over the shoulders; it is in
general very handsomely embroidered with various coloured
ribbons, particularly green or yellow; under this they wear
a cloth dress, not unlike a European riding-habit. When
going abroad, they wear a black beaver-hat, ornamented with
feathers and bands of various-coloured ribbons. On the entire, an Indian woman, in her Sunday-dress, has a very pretty
and interesting appearance.

Their canoes differ considerably from those of the Esquimeaux, as well in the shape as in the materials of which they
are formed. The American canoe is completely open at top,
and is made of sections of bark, taken from the birch-tree ;
these are sewed together with filaments from the roots of the
spruce fir-tree, called *watape.* They are about thirty feet in
length, and about six in breadth at the widest part. The
bottom is rounded, and they have no keel. The frame is
formed of slight pieces of light wood, over which is fastened
a sheathing composed of the materials already mentioned.
Instead of the double paddle, used by the Esquimeaux, they
make use of a short piece of wood, about three feet long,
narrow at the top, and gradually becoming broad towards the
extremity ; on the whole, not unlike the extremity of an English oar cut off.

The manner in which they construct their tents, or wigwams, is as follows : Being provided with poles of a proper
length, they fasten two of them across, near the ends, with
bands made of birch rind ; having done this, they raise them
up, and extend the lower part of each as wide as they propose to make the area of the tent; other poles, of an equal
height, are then set round at equal distances from each other,

so that their lower ends form a complete circle ; over the entire is spread the tent-cloth, which is generally made of deer-skins* dressed by the natives. A slit is made in the bottom part, which serves the purpose of door ; it is always placed opposite to that point from which the wind blows. These tents have neither window nor chimney; there is merely an aperture left in the middle of the roof, which serves the double purpose of letting out the smoke, and admitting the light.

This humble wigwam constitutes the entire of a North-American Indian's residence, serving him as kitchen, parlour, bed-room, &c. In one part, their culinary and domestic utensils are arranged ; in another, their beds, which are rolled up during the day, and covered with a large buffaloe-skin ; and in another, the materials for their work. Among their culinary utensils is what they term a skippertogan, or small bag, which contains a flint, steel, and touchwood. Some of these bags are uncommonly handsome, being richly ornamented with beads, porcupine-quills, and ermine. The perogan, or tinder, the Indians make use of, is a kind of fungus that grows on the outside of the birch-tree. There are two kinds, one hard, and not unlike rhubarb ; the other soft and smooth. The latter is prepared for use by laying it on hot ashes, and then reducing it to a state of fine powder. The hard kind is very easily ignited, catching even the smallest spark that falls from the steel ; once on fire, it is very difficult to extinguish it ; the spark appears to spread and burrow through the entire mass in all directions, so that, though to all appearance it is quite extinguished, combustion is all the time going on internally ; hence the use of it is attended with considerable risk. I have had pieces of it in my pocket quite free, as I conceived, from combustion ; on putting in my hand, however, I have frequently found the entire reduced almost to a cinder. In the interior, where they have no opportunity of getting a flint and steel, they procure fire by rubbing two smooth pieces of wood rapidly against each other.

---

* The Indian mode of dressing leather is as follows: A lather is made of the brains and some of the soft fat or marrow of the animal commonly called the rein-deer ; in this the skin is well soaked, when it is taken out, and not only dried by the heat of a fire, but hung up in the smoke for several days; it is then taken down, and is well soaked and washed in warm water till the grain of the skin is perfectly open, and it has imbibed a sufficient quantity of water ; after which it is taken out, and wrung as dry as possible, and then dried by the heat of a slow fire, care being taken to rub and stretch it as long as any moisture remains in the skin ; afterwards they are scraped to make them quite smooth.—*See* HERON'S *Voyage up Coppermine River.*—Being dressed in oil, they always grow harder after being wet, unless great care be taken to keep rubbing them all the time they are drying.

Those situated about the factory boil their victuals in tin or copper vessels, which they procure in exchange for furs. Those at a distance from it are, however, obliged to substitute vessels made of the bark of the birch-tree, sewed together with some vegetable fibre. As they will not bear exposure to the fire sufficient to bring water to a boiling temperature, they are obliged to have recourse to the following contrivance : they take some large stones, and place them in the centre of the fire until they are red-hot; they then take them out, and plunge them into the birch-rind vessel. By continuing this process for some time, the water is soon brought to a state of ebullition. The food, however, when dressed in this way, is generally mixed with sand, or small particles of gravel.

The care of their tents is consigned entirely to the women; as is, indeed, all the drudgery of an Indian life. They are obliged, while travelling, to pitch their tents, dress their victuals, make and repair every article of dress. In short, the moment she becomes a wife she loses her liberty, and is an obsequious slave to her husband, who takes good care never to lose sight of his prerogative. Wherever he goes she must follow, and durst not venture to incense him by a refusal, knowing that if she neglects him, extreme punishment, if not death, ensues. Notwithstanding all this, they are generally found humble and faithful servants,* tender and affectionate wives, fond and indulgent parents. I have frequently gone into their tents, and have sat for hours delighted and amused with their modest unassuming manners, and simple habits of humble industry. On going in, they always offered me some dried buffaloe-tongue, or perhaps some pimmicum,† an article

---

* In every part of the world, one of the most general characteristics of the savage is to despise and degrade the female sex. Among most of the tribes in America, their condition is so peculiarly grievous, that servitude is a name too mild to describe their wretched state ; a wife is no better than a beast of burden. While the man passes his days in idleness or amusement, the woman is condemned to incessant toil. Tasks are imposed upon her without mercy, and services are received without complacence or gratitude. There are some districts in America, where this state of degradation has been so severely felt, that mothers have destroyed their female infants to deliver them at once from a life in which they were doomed to such a miserable slavery.—*See* MALTHUS *on Population.*

† The provision called pimmicum is prepared in the following manner : The lean parts of the flesh of the larger animals are cut in thin slices, and are placed on a wooden grate over a slow fire, or exposed to the sun, and sometimes to the frost. By these operations it is dried, and in that state is pounded between two stones so as to reduce it to a fine powder ; it is then made into cakes, which will keep for almost any length of time.

of diet on which they principally subsist during their journies into the interior.

The character I have here given applies principally to the northern Indian women, as the southern Indian females are, I have been informed, a most profligate abandoned set. Like every other class of people, however, there are exceptions. Amongst them, Mr. Hearne, in his interesting work, gives the following very remarkable one :—

Mary, the daughter of Moses Norton, a native of the country, and for many years chief at Prince of Wales's Fort, in Hudson's Bay, though born and brought up in a country of all others the least favourable to virtue and to virtuous principles, possessed these and every other good and amiable quality in the most eminent degree. Without the assistance of religion, and with no education but what she received among the dissolute natives of her country, she would have shone with superior lustre in any community; for if an engaging person, gentle manners, an easy freedom, arising from a consciousness of innocence; an amiable modesty, and an unrivalled delicacy of sentiment, are graces and virtues which render a woman lovely, none ever had greater pretensions to esteem and regard; while her benevolence, humanity, and scrupulous adherence to truth, would have done honour to the most enlightened and devout christian. Dutiful, obedient, and affectionate to her parents, steady and faithful to her friends, grateful and humble to her benefactors ; easily forgiving and forgetting injuries, careful not to offend any, and courteous and kind to all ; she was nevertheless suffered to perish by the rigours of cold and hunger, amidst her own relations, at a time when the griping hand of famine was by no means severely felt by any other member of their company; and it may truly be said, that she fell a martyr to the principles of virtue. This happened in the winter of the year 1782, after the French had destroyed Prince of Wales's Fort, at which time she was in the 22d year of her age. Human nature shudders at the bare recital of such brutality, and reason shrinks from the task of accounting for the decrees of Providence on such occasions as this ; but they are the strongest assurances of a future state, so infinitely superior to the present, that the enjoyment of every pleasure in this world, by the most worthless and abandoned wretch, or the most innocent and virtuous woman, perishing by the most excruciating of all deaths, are matters equally indifferent ; but—

Peace to the ashes and the virtuous mind
Of her who liv'd in peace with all mankind ;

Learn'd from the heart, unknowing of disguise;
Truth in her thoughts, and candour in her eyes;
Stranger alike to envy and to pride,
Good sense her light, and nature all her guide;
But now remov'd from all the ills of life,
Here rests the pleasing friend and faithful wife!

WALLER.

The speed and facility with which the Indian women pass
through the most interesting period of female suffering, has
long been a matter of observation, and of surprise. A very
remarkable instance of this occurred during my stay at York
Fort, which I shall here take the liberty to mention. Mrs.
B., an Indian lady, wife of one of the inland governors, was
occupied the entire day about her tent. I entered her tent at
three o'clock in the afternoon; she was then preparing dinner,
which consisted of boiled venison, venison-soup, and English
biscuit; she was at that time quite cheerful, and in remarkably good spirits. About six o'clock in the evening she was
seized with labour-pains, when she retired to an apartment in
the governor's house, in company with an elderly Indian woman; about half-past six she was delivered of a fine boy; and
a little after seven of the same evening, I saw her walking
about the factory. The young infant immediately born was
washed with cold-water, and afterwards wrapped up in a
young beaver-skin and placed in its cradle, which is made as
follows: They take a plain piece of board, about three feet
long and one and a half in breadth; to either side of this they
make fast a portion of cloth or ticking, which they procure
from the Europeans; this they adorn with beads and quill-
work, in a very tasty and beautiful manner. Under this outer
covering, which is made to lace up the front, they place a fine
English blanket, folded in a circular form, and inside of this
they place a layer of very fine moss, for the purpose of absorb-
ing the discharges of the child; when soiled it is immediately
renewed. To each corner of the flat piece of board a string
is attached, which terminates in a loop: by these they are suspended from the side of the tent, so as not to prevent them
attending to their work. To one end of the board a broad
worsted belt is made fast; when travelling this is passed round
the forehead, while the cradle hangs behind. The face of the
child is all that is seen, the arms and feet being confined under
the cloths and bandages which are wrapped round it. In
summer a piece of gauze is thrown over the young savage, to
keep off the musquitos, which are at this season very troublesome. Shortly after the child was born it was given the breast;
I could not help admiring the tender and affectionate looks

this fond mother gave her little babe while she was giving it this nourishment, or, as they very beautifully express it, tootooshonarto, the *sap of the human breast.* The day following that of which I have been speaking, Mrs. B. and her husband set out on a journey of two hundred miles.

Long, in his account of the North American Indians, relates the following anecdote : " About an hour before sun-set, on the fourth day, we stopped at a small creek, which was too deep to be forded, and whilst the Indian was assisting me in making a raft to cross over, rather than swim through in such cold weather against a strong current, I looked round and missed his wife; I was rather displeased, as the sun was near setting, and I was anxious to gain the opposite shore to encamp before dark. I asked the Indian where his wife was gone; he smiled, and told me, he supposed into the woods to set a collar for a partridge. In about an hour she returned with a new-born infant in her arms, and coming up to me said in Chippeway, ' Oway Sagonnash Payshik Skomagonish,' or, here Englishman is a young warrior." Mr. Hearne informs us, that when a northern Indian woman is taken in labour, a small tent is erected for her, at such a distance from the other tents that her cries cannot easily be heard, and the other women and young girls are her constant attendants. No male, except children in arms, are ever allowed to approach her. It is a circumstance, perhaps, to be lamented, that these people never attempt to assist each other on these occasions, even in the most critical cases. This is in some measure owing to delicacy, but more probably to an opinion they entertain, that nature is abundantly sufficient to perform every thing required without any external helps whatever. Mr. Hearne tells us, that when he informed them of the assistance which European women derive from the skill and attention of practitioners in midwifery, they treated it with the utmost contempt, ironically observing, " that the many hump-backs, bandy-legs, and other deformities, so frequent among the English, were undoubtedly owing to the great skill of the persons who assisted in bringing them into the world, and to the extraordinary care of the nurses afterwards."

After childbirth an Indian woman is reckoned unclean for a month or five weeks, during which time she always remains in a small tent placed at a little distance from the others, with only a female acquaintance or two ; and during the whole time the father never sees the child. The reason which they assign for this practice is, that children when first born are sometimes not very sightly, having in general large heads and but little hair, and are, moreover, often discoloured by the force of

labour;* so that were the father to see them to such great dis-
advantage, he might, probably, take a dislike to them, which
never afterwards could be removed. It is said, that when delivered of twins, they sacrifice that which appears to them the
weaker of the two ; this monstrous practice exists among many
wandering nations, where the men never take any burdens
that might encumber them in the chace. They generally
suckle their children for two years ; some, however, continue
it for three, four, and even five years.

The absolute want of all kind of domestic cattle, and consequently the total want of all milk-diet, is the principal reason
why the American women keep their infants so long a time at
the breast. It is probably owing to this long-continued nurs-
ing that the mammæ are in them so relaxed and pendulous.†
They are, however, by no means so long as some writers
would lead us to suppose ; indeed, I suspect there is much
exaggeration, if not absolute falsehood, in some of these narra-
tions. Thus, in Hakluyt's Collection, vol. ii. p. 26, it is
asserted, that divers women have such exceeding long breasts
that some of them will lay the same upon the ground, and lie
down by them. Bruce asserts, that in some of the Shangallas
they hang down to the knees. Mentzelius tells us, that purses
are made in great numbers from the breasts of Hottentot females, and sold at the Cape of Good Hope. But what will
appear still more extraordinary is, that the females of this
country (Ireland) have been accused of this extreme pendulous state of the mammæ. I hope my fair country-women
will excuse me for making the following extract: Lithgow,
in his " Raire Adventures and Painefulle Pergrinations," p.
433, says, " I saw, in Ireland's northe parts, women travayl-
ing the way, or toyling at home, carry their infants about their
neckes, and laying the dugges over their shoulders ; would
give sucke to the babes behinde their backs, without taking
them in their armes. Such kind of breasts, me thinketh, were
very fit to be made money-bags for East or West-Indian mer-
chants, being more than half a yard long, and as well wrought
as any tanner, in the like charge, could ever mollifie such
leather."

---

* We are not, however, to suppose that this process is so readily accomplished in all cases. Mr. Fidler informed me, that they are somtimes a day
and a night in labour. In this case they frequently pass a stick horizontally
along the abdomen, for the purpose of exciting uterine contraction. If travelling, they place the child on their backs and resume their journey.

† See Article Man, Rees Cyclopædia.

The Indian women are remarkably attached to their young charge,* watching over them with the greatest affection and tenderness ; and, should they die, lamenting their loss in the most affecting manner. Even for several months after their decease they visit their little graves, and shed over them some very bitter tears. From their infant state they endeavour to promote an independent spirit in their offspring ; they are never known either to beat or scold them, lest the martial disposition which is to adorn their future life and character should be weakened. On all occasions they avoid every thing compulsive, that the freedom with which they wish them to act may not be controuled. They instruct them in lessons of patience and fortitude, and endeavour to inspire them with courage in war, and a contempt of danger and death ; above all things, they endeavour to instil into their minds an hereditary hatred and implacable thirst of revenge towards the Esquimeaux.

The North American Indians, in general, have five or six wives. Indeed, this is frequently the only mark of distinction amongst them, that man being most respected who is best able to support the greatest number of women. Thus Matonnabee, an Indian chief, who conducted Mr. Hearne up Coppermine River, had eight of them. Their names are generally taken from some part or property of a beaver, martin, or other animal. When they wish to take a wife, and that they find one to their mind, the Indian applies to the father of the girl, and asks his consent in the following words :

" Nocey, Cunner kee darmissey kee darniss nee zargay-

---

* A singular instance of this occurred during Mr. Ellis's residence at York Fort. Two small canoes passing Hayes's River, when they had got to the middle of it, one of them, which was made of the bark of a birch-tree, sunk, in which was an Indian, his wife, and child. The other canoe being small, and incapable of receiving more than one of the parents and the child, produced a very extraordinary contest between the man and his wife, not but that both of them were willing to devote themselves to save the other; but that the difficulty lay in determining which would be the greatest loss to the child. The man used many arguments to prove it more reasonable that he should be drowned than the woman. But she alledged, on the contrary, it was more for the advantage of the child that she should perish, because he, as a man, was better to hunt, and consequently to provide for it. The little time there was still remaining was spent in mutual expressions of tenderness, the woman strongly recommending, as for the last time, to her husband, the care of her child. This being done, they took leave in the water; the woman quitting the canoe was drowned, and the man with the child got safe ashore, and is now taken much notice of by the people thereabouts.— *See Ellis's Voyage to Hudson's Bay,* p. 88.

gar kakaygo o waterwarwardoossin cawween peccan weeley
ganunat ottertassey memarjis mee mor."

"Father, I love your daughter ; will you give her to me, that
the small roots of her heart may entangle with mine, so that
the strongest wind that blows shall never separate them." If
the father approves, an interview is appointed, for which the
lover prepares by a perspiration ; he then comes into her presence, sits down on the ground and smokes his pipe ; during
the time of smoking he continues throwing small pieces of
wood of about an inch in length at her, one by one, to the
number of a hundred. As many as she can catch in a bark
bowl, so many presents her lover must make to her father,
which the latter considers as payment for his daughter. The
young warrior then gives a feast, to which he invites all the
family. When the feast is done, they sing and dance to their
war-songs.

The merriment being over, and mutual presents exchanged
between the lover and her relations, the father covers them
with a beaver robe, and gives them, likewise, a gun and birch
canoe, with which the ceremony ends.

Conjuring is a very common practice among them, and is
frequently had recourse to for the purpose of procuring respect and distinction. As the conjurors are the only persons
applied to in bodily ailments, their deceptious practices are
also resorted to for the purpose of spreading their professional
fame. Frequently they get themselves bound up in the following manner : Being stripped quite naked, cords are passed
round each finger, and then over the entire hand, so as to de-
prive them altogether of the power of moving these parts ;
they are then fastened behind their backs ; a large buffaloe
skin is now thrown over them, and is tied round with ropes,
beginning from above downwards. The legs are secured in
a similar manner, so that they are deprived of the least power
of motion. Bound up in this manner they are put into a tent
alone ; after extricating themselves they come out, and tell the
by-standers exultingly, that it was the great spirit that assisted
them in getting free. When a relation or friend to whom they
are particularly attached is, as they suppose, in extreme danger, they make use of the most absurd superstitious practices,
such as pretending to swallow knives, chissels, hatchets, &c.
This is done from a superstitious notion, that they will be able,
by these means, to appease the " old scythe-man," and thus
procure a respite for their patient. When these extraordinary
practices are had recourse to, the patient is placed in the middle of a small square tent, and in a short time is followed by

the conjuror, who is stripped quite naked. In very hopeless cases they call for consultation ; in this case the assistants also enter quite naked. Having closed the door of the tent very accurately, they then arrange themselves about the unfortunate patient, and begin to suck and blow at the parts affected,* and in a short time to sing and talk, as if conversing with familiar spirits, which they pretend appear to them in the shape of different animals. After a long conference with those invisible agents, they then call for the instrument which they are to swallow. They very prudently have a long string attached to this knife, bayonet, or whatever else it may be, for the purpose of drawing it up again. After having practiced this deception several times, they again commence sucking the part affected. After this the surating process is commenced ; for this purpose the tent is closed as accurately as possible on all sides. Red-hot stones are then thrown into a vessel of water, and in a short time the whole tent is filled with steam, which, acting on the surface of the skin, soon produces a copious sweat. This being continued until a feeling of weakness is induced, the cure is then said to be completed ; and certainly it must be allowed, especially where the complaint is of a rheumatic description, that this is not unfrequently the case. Mr. Hearne, in the interesting work already so often alluded to, gives the following very curious instances of which he was himself an eye-witness. " At the time when the forty and odd tents of Indians joined us, one man was so dangerously ill that it was thought necessary the conjurors should use some of their wonderful experiments for his recovery ; one of them, therefore, immediately consented to swallow a broad bayonet. Accordingly a conjuring-house was erected, into which the patient was conveyed, and he was soon followed by the conjuror, who, after a long preparatory discourse, and the necessary conference with the familiar spirits, advanced to the door and asked for the bayonet, which was then ready prepared by having a string fastened to it, and a short piece of wood tied to the other end of the string to prevent him swallowing it.

---

* For some inward complaints, such as griping in the intestines, &c., it is very common to see those jugglers blowing into the rectum until their eyes are almost starting out of their head. The accumulation of so large a quantity of wind is, at times, apt to occasion some extraordinary emotions, which are not easily suppressed by a sick person ; and, as there is no vent for it but the channel through which it was conveyed thither, it sometimes occasions an odd scene between the doctor and his patient, which I once wantonly called an engagement ; but for which I was afterwards exceedingly sorry, as it highly offended several of the Indians, particularly the juggler and sick person.—*Hearne's Voyage up Coppermine River.*

Though I am not so credulous," continues Mr. Hearne, " as to believe, that the conjuror absolutely swallowed the bayonet, yet I must acknowledge, that, in the twinkling of an eye, he conveyed it to —— God knows where; and the small piece of wood, or one exactly like it, was confined close to his teeth. He then paraded backward and forward before the conjuring-house for a short time, when he feigned to be greatly disordered in his stomach and bowels; and, after making many wry-faces and groaning most hideously, he put his body into several distorted attitudes, very suitable to the occasion.   He then returned to the door of the conjuring-house, and, after making strong efforts to vomit, by the help of the string he, at length, and after tugging at it for some time, produced the bayonet, which apparently he hauled out of his mouth, to the no small surprize of all present.   He then looked round with an air of exultation, and strutted into the conjuring-house, where he renewed his incantations, and continued them without intermission for twenty-four hours."   The other instance which Mr. Hearne mentions, is that of a poor paralytic Indian, who had been in a most deplorable condition for a length of time.   " That nothing," remarks Mr. Hearne, " might be wanting towards his recovery, the same man who deceived me in swallowing a bayonet in the summer, now offered to swallow a large piece of board, about the size of a barrel-stave, in order to effect his recovery.   The piece of board was prepared by another man, and painted according to the directions of the juggler, with a rude representation of some beast of prey on one side; and on the reverse was painted, according to their rude method, a resemblance of the sky.   After holding the necessary conference with the invisible spirits, he asked if I was present, for he had heard of my saying that I did not see him swallow the bayonet fair; and, on being answered in the affirmative, he desired me to come nearer; on which the Indians made a lane for me to pass, and I advanced close to him, and found him standing at the conjuring-house door as naked as when born.   When the piece of board was delivered to him he proposed at first only to shove one-third of it down his throat, and then walk round the company; afterwards to shove down another third, and so proceed till he had swallowed the whole, except a small piece of the end, which was to be left behind for the purpose of hauling it up again.   When he put it to his mouth it apparently slipped down his throat like lightning, and only left about three inches sticking without his lips; after walking backwards and forwards three times, he hauled it up again, and ran into the conjuring-house with great precipitation.   This he did, to all appearance, with great care and composure, and, notwithstanding I was all attention on the occasion, I could not detect the deceit: and as to the reality of its being a piece of wood that he pretended to swallow, there is not the least reason to doubt, for I had it in my hand both before and immediately after the ceremony."

Matonnabee, an Indian chief, who was then present, assured Mr. Hearne that he had seen a man, who was then in company, swallow a child's cradle with as much ease as he could fold up a piece of paper, and put it into his mouth; and that when he hauled it up again, not the mark of a tooth, or of any violence, was discovered about it. It is really extremely difficult, and oftentimes altogether impossible to give any satisfactory explanation of the manner in which these feats of legerdemain are accomplished. I may remark, however, and, indeed, Mr. Hearne admits the fact, that in the second instance there was great room for deception. Though the conjuror was quite naked, he had several of his companions well clothed standing very close round him during the entire ceremony, and to whom he probably slipped the main piece of wood. This suspicion is confirmed by the circumstance of Mr. Hearne having seen this man on that very day shape a piece of wood of precisely the same figure as that which protruded from the mouth, which was of this ⟨ shape. The figure of the entire piece was nearly what is here represented ▭▭▭▭⟨. It is probable, therefore, that the top part was merely inserted into the body of the stave, so that it could be removed at pleasure.

They rarely have recourse to any medicines either for their internal or external complaints, generally trusting for relief to such nonsensical charms as I have described. Sometimes, however, especially after their drunken freaks, they make use of blood-letting, which is performed in the following manner: they take a small sharp instrument, not unlike an awl, and drive it into the flesh under the vein which it is proposed to open; they then cut down on the vessel with a common knife. Those who have neither of the instruments mentioned, make use of a sharp flint, with which they divide the vein.

Lambert, in his travels through the United States of North-America, assures us, that they frequently, especially when after a fit of intoxication, quaff off, while yet quite warm, the blood which has been drawn from the arm of another Indian. In the year 1801, while travelling across the rocky mountains of the north-west, Mr. Lambert had an opportunity of witnessing this disgusting sight. " This morning our guide, belonging to the Cree tribe, complained that his head and stomach were out of order, owing to the excess of last night, and asked for a little medicine, which was given to him; but finding it did him neither good nor harm, he called his wife to him, where he was sitting amongst us at a large fire we had made to warm ourselves. She readily came: he asked her if she had a sharp flint? and upon her replying that she had not, he broke one, and made a lancet of it, with which he opened a vein in his wife's arm, she assisting him with great good-will. Having drawn about a pint of blood from her in a wooden bowl, to our astonishment he applied it to his mouth quite warm, and drank it off; he then mixed the blood that adhered to the vessel with water, by way of cleansing the bowl, and also drank that off. While I was considering the savageness of this action, one of our men, with indignation, exclaimed to our guide, " I have eaten and smoked with thee: but henceforward thou and I shall not smoke and eat together. What! drink, warm from the vein, the blood of thy wife !"— " Oh, my friend," said the Indian, " have I done wrong? When I find my stomach out of order, the warm blood of my wife, in good health, refreshes the whole of my body, and puts me to rights: in return, when she is not well, I draw blood from my arm, she drinks it, and it gives her life. All our nation do the same, and they all know it to be a good medicine."

Mr. Ellis tells us, that for the purpose of curing cholic, and all bowel complaints, they swallow a large quantity of tobacco-smoke, by which they positively affirm they obtain great and speedy relief. I can hardly think they use pure tobacco on those occasions; it is in all probability mixed with a plant which they are very fond of smoking, called sackasshiapuk.

No people indulge in sorrow to such an excess as the North-American Indians. Many of them, when they lose a friend or near relation, think nothing of cutting and mangling themselves in a most shocking manner. Very frequently some pass a knife through the fleshy part* of the thigh or arm; others cut off a joint of a finger for each relation they have lost; others, again, pluck the nail out by the root, and lap

---

* That these practices were usual among the heathens so early as the days of Moses, is evident from the injunction which the Lord laid on the children of Israel to avoid them. " You shall not round the corners of your head, neither shall you mar the corners of thy beard. You shall not make any cuttings in your flesh for the dead, nor print any marks upon you."* And again, " Ye are the children of the Lord your God; you shall not cut yourselves, nor make any baldness between your eyes for the dead."†

down the top of the finger. I recollect Mr. Swaine, one of the inland governors, mentioning to me that a Bungee woman came to his house last winter. Observing that she had several joints of her fingers cut off, he enquired of her the cause; when she immediately burst into tears, and told him, that for each of those joints she had lost a relative. It is probable, that these horrible practices are resorted to under the impression that the malignant powers delight in groans and misery, and that they are not to be appeased but by human blood.

When about to depart this life, they meet their approaching fate with firmness and resignation; not unfrequently, indeed, especially when advanced in life,* they long for the expected summons. " It is better," said an aged Indian, " to be seated than standing; to be asleep than awake: to be dead than alive." After putting on their best clothes, the family is called around, and addressed in a firm manly tone, exhorting them to lead peaceable industrious lives; to be obliging and friendly towards the Europeans; and if they bear any revenge towards another tribe, they are exhorted to carry it to the last. He endures his tortures with the greatest composure; tells them he is going to the land of spirits, that blissful abode where he will have plenty of fowling and fishing; and desires them to bury with him his gun, shot-pouch, kettle, as also his skippertoggan, containing his flint, steel, and touch-wood. All this is faithfully complied with. If, however, they should at any time stand much in need of any of these articles, as a gun, for instance, they very often take it from their graves, and leave in its place a long pole.

With regard to their religious sentiments, there is, I believe, but little difference. They all believe in a great good Being, and in a great bad one. They generally pray to the bad one that he may not injure them; to the good one they think it unnecessary to pray, as they are confident he will not injure

---

* One custom they have, which is very extraordinary: When their parents grow so old as to be incapable of supporting themselves by their own labour, they require their children to strangle them, and this is esteemed an act of obedience in them to perform. The manner of discharging this last duty is thus: the grave of the old person being dug, he goes into it; and, after having conversed, and smoked a pipe, or perhaps drank a dram or two with his children, the old person signifies that he is ready; upon which two of the children put a thong about his neck, one standing on one side, and the other opposite to him, pull violently till he is strangled, then cover him with earth, and over that they erect a kind of rough monument of stones. Such persons as have no children, request this office from their friends; though, in this last case, it is not always complied with.—*See* ELLIS's *Voyage to Hudson's Bay.*

them. Their opinion of the origin of mankind is, that the Great Spirit made the first men and women out of the earth, three in number of each; that those whom we Europeans sprang from were made from a whiter earth than what their progenitors were; and that there was one pair of still blacker earth than that from which they were formed. Almost all of them believe in a future state of rewards and punishments, but unhappily they have blended with these important truths the most puerile and extravagant fancies, which are neither founded on rational piety, or productive of moral obligation.

The climate here is almost always wintry; the hot weather, though violent, being of very short duration. About October, the snow begins to appear, and continues to fall at intervals the entire winter. During this season, the thermometer is often known to fall fifty degrees below the freezing point. Wine is said to freeze into a solid mass; and brandy to assume a coagulated form;* even the breath is said to fall in the form of hoar-frost upon the blankets. Frozen mercury has been reduced to plates as thin as paper, by beating it on an anvil previously reduced to the same temperature. When put into a glass of warm-water, a curious appearance is observed: the water instantly becomes solid, while the mercury passes to the fluid state. By the rapidity of the action, the glass in which it was immersed was shivered into a thousand pieces.

During this season, the inhabitants live principally in tents, constructed after the manner already mentioned, the sides of which are covered with snow for the purpose of increasing their warmth. Frequently, for weeks together, no one dare venture out, without running great risk of their lives.

> " Nought around
> Strikes his sad eye, but deserts lost in snow.
> And heavy loaded groves, and solid floods,
> That stretch athwart the solitary vast
> Their icy horrors to the frozen main."†

---

* If in drinking a dram of brandy out of a glass, one's tongue or lips touch it, in pulling them away the skin is left upon it. An odd instance of this sort happened to one of our people who was carrying a bottle of spirits from the house to his tent; for, not having a cork to stop the bottle, he made use of his finger, which was soon frozen fast, by which accident he lost a part of it to make a cure practicable.

† If a door or window was but opened, the cold air rushed in with great fury, and turned the inclosed vapours into small snow. Nor was all the heat we could raise sufficient to keep our windows, the ceiling, or sides of the house, clear from snow or ice. Those whose bed-clothes touched the walls, were generally froze fast to them by morning; and our breaths settled in a white hoar-frost upon the blankets.—*See* ELLIS's *Voyage to Hudson's Bay,* p. 81.

At this time they subsist principally on salted geese, dried tongues, and pimmicum. When the weather is more moderate, however, they hunt the rein-deer, which they often meet in vast herds, seeking the extreme cold. Frequently, they merely take out the tongues, leaving the rest of the body to putrify, or to be devoured by wild beasts. At times, however, such is the extreme scarcity of food, that they are obliged to have recourse to the most filthy and disgusting practices for the purpose of sustaining life. Many are obliged to strip the hair from the peltry which they are bringing to the different factories, and subsist on the skins. Others procure a scanty nourishment from the deer-skins, with which their shoes and other parts of their dress are formed; and, at times, such is the dreadful want of provisions, that they are compelled to resort to the horrid and revolting practice of cannibalism. Mr. Swaine mentioned to me an instance which occurred the preceding winter, of a southern Indian woman, who was in such extreme want, that she dug up one of her own relatives, who had been some time buried, and fed for several days on this shocking repast.

Mr. Ellis tells us " that an Indian, who with his family was coming down to trade from a place very far distant, had the misfortune to meet with but little game by the way; so that in a short time himself, his wife, and his children, were reduced to the last distress. In these circumstances, they plucked the fur from their clothes, and preserved life as long as they were able, by feeding on the skins which they wore; but even this wretched resource soon failed them; and then, what is terrible to conceive, and horrible to relate, these poor creatures sustained themselves by feeding on two of their children."

Mr. Hearne, in p. 85 of his interesting work, makes mention of the following instance: " In the spring of the year 1775, when I was building Cumberland-house, an Indian, whose name was Wappoos, came to the settlement at a time when fifteen tents of Indians were on the plantations; they examined him very minutely, and found he had come a considerable way by himself, without a gun or ammunition. This made many of them conjecture he had met with and killed some person by the way; and this was the more easily credited, from the care he took to conceal a bag of provisions which he had brought with him in a lofty pine-tree near the house. Being a stranger, I invited him in, though I saw he had nothing for trade; and, during that interview, some of the Indian women examined his bag, and gave it as their opinion that the meat it contained was human flesh; in consequence, it was not without the interference of some principal Indians, whose liberality of sentiment was more extensive than in the others, that the poor creature's life was saved. Many of the men cleaned and loaded their guns; others had their bows and arrows ready; and even the women took possession of the hatchets, to kill this poor inoffensive creature, for no crime but that of travelling about 200 miles by himself, unassisted by fire-arms for his support on his journey."

It is asserted that the southern Indians, if once they are driven to this unnatural practice, become so fond of it that no person is safe in their company. They are, however, despised and neglected for ever after.

From the instances which I have here related, particularly that by Mr. Hearne, we may conclude that cannibalism has always originated in extreme want, though it may afterwards be continued from other motives.

During this frightful season, the whole animal creation, instead of the usual variety which exists during the summer, puts on the " winter robe of purest white." Even animals which have been brought from this country become, at this period, of a milk-white colour. It is a difficult matter to say what purposes in the animal economy this singular change may serve. It once occurred to me, that perhaps a white surface might possess less radiating powers, and in this way preserve to the animal body a quantity of caloric, which would otherwise be dissipated by the intense cold of the climate. I found, however, that on placing a canister, constructed after Mr. Lesslie's directions, and on which I had pasted portions of different coloured skins in the focus of a concave mirror, that there was not the slightest difference in the effects produced on the differential thermometer. There is, in fact, but little known of a satisfactory nature on this interesting subject; I shall, therefore, drop it here, lest, by substituting conjecture in the place of more solid information, I might disgust the sensible reader. Another change is observed to take place in the animal creation at this time, the wise intentions of which are sufficiently obvious: the skin of every animal is covered with a finer and longer fur* than they possessed dur-

---

* A corresponding change, we find, takes place in warm climates. Thus the sheep in Africa has a *coarse* hair substituted in place of its wool; and the dog loses its coat entirely, and has a smooth and soft skin. Goats also undergo a considerable alteration. A person unacquainted with this change, would hardly believe that the Cashmere shawls, which are sold at such an enormous high price, could be the produce of that animal.—REES's *Cyclop.*

ing the summer; thus the clothing of each is admirably adapted to the rigours of its situation. The fox and the wolf, which in temperate climates have but comparatively short hair, in these frozen regions are covered with a fine, long, and thick fur. The beaver and the ermine, which are found in the greatest abundance in these high latitudes, are remarkable for the warmth and delicacy of their furs. It is owing to these changes that the peltry of northern climes are so much admired, and so highly valued.

About May, nature again resumes her wonted liberty ; the ice begins to drift away, the snows to dissolve, and the animals to resume their usual variety of colour. About June the hot weather commences ; and, in a short time, the heat is so intense as to scorch the face of the natives. A rapid and luxurious vegetation now sets in; so that, in a short time, instead of the waste and dreary appearance which but a little before presented itself, the eye is refreshed with a rich and beautiful verdure. This change, indeed, is so rapid, that it is probably going on for a considerable time before the snows melt away. Even in this country I have frequently observed, that when heavy snow has fallen at the close of a long and severe winter, it has been pushed off, as it were, by the young shoots projecting themselves through it; and this, though the temperature of the air was below 32°. It is very likely, indeed, that but for this covering, vegetation would have been considerably retarded.

The remarkable increase of heat which is observed here, during the summer months, is owing, in a great measure, to the length of time the sun remains above the horizon ; thus compensating for the shortness of its stay, as also to the slowness with which an equilibrium of temperature, by the circulation of the atmosphere, takes place. Its excess, however, is moderated by the large quantity of caloric which those immense masses of ice and snow absorb while passing to the fluid form. I may also remark, that the rigour of winter must also be considerably mitigated by the warmth evolved, as congelation again begins to spread over those dreary retreats.

Dr. Darwin tells us, that it was in consequence of the want of this protection that many Lapland and Alpine plants perished in the botanic garden at Upsal, although the cold was not more intense than what prevails for a great part of the year in their native situations ; but in those climates, the fall of snow commonly commences with the diminished temperature of the season, and in this manner it affords a protection to the vegetable tribes against the increasing coldness of the weather. There are even many plants,* particularly lichens and mosses, which thrive only in the coldest climates, and continue to live when the thermometer is many degrees below 0 of Fahrenheit. Besides the protective covering which the snow affords, they are also enabled to resist this extreme, by means of the power † which they possess, in common with all organized beings, of preserving a certain temperature independent of external circumstances.

During the several excursions which I made into the woods while on shore, I have gathered a considerable quantity of gooseberries, currants, and strawberries. Cranberries are also to be found in great abundance. The gooseberries were very large, and of a remarkably fine flavour; they are all red, at least I never saw any others; the bushes are in every respect similar to those of this country, but that they are much lower, seldom exceeding two feet high. The currants were very fine; both red and black appeared very abundant; the latter, however, are said to be the most plentiful. American strawberries are called by the Indians ooteagh minik, from their resemblance to a heart; their flavour is delicious, much superior, I think, to that produced by cultivation. The cranberry found here appears to belong to the species *vaccinium macrocurpon.* The following are its characters: corolla pink, deeply four-cleft: leaves elliptic, oblong, entire, slightly revolute, obtuse, smooth: stems ascending: flowers lateral, filaments purple, downy: anthers yellow, converging, without spurs: the germen is smooth: the berry is pear-shaped, crimson, and of a peculiar flavour. We packed a large quantity of them in small casks, and used them on the passage; they made remarkably nice pies. Sir Joseph Banks advises us, in order to have this species of cranberry, to cultivate it in an artificial bog, with plenty of water. He assures us, that a few square yards of ground occupied in this way, will yield as many cranberries as any family can use.

I shall here give an account of the other plants which I

---

* Thus (the lichen langiferinus) coral moss vegetates beneath the snow in Siberia, where the degree of heat is always about 40°, that is, in the medium between the freezing point and the common heat of the earth. This vegetable is for many months of the winter the sole food of the rein-deer; who digs furrows in the snow, and scrapes it up; and as the milk and flesh of this animal are almost the only sustenance which can be procured by the natives during the long winters of those high latitudes, this moss may be said to support millions of mankind.—*See* DARWIN's *Zoonomia.*

† Hence the common observation that snow is for a long time dissolved on hedges before it disappears from the neighbouring path-way.

collected during these excursions. The most abundant is the sorrel, belonging to the species *oxalis stricta*, or yellow upright wood-sorrel. The root is creeping: stem erect, branched: leaflets inversely heart-shaped : umbels stalked : axillary : solitary : many-flowered. The flowers are numerous, small, yellow : *stamens* covered with a downy substance.

Coltsfoot is also very common : it appeared to belong to the species *tupilago sagittata.* The flowers were radiated, and of a light flesh-colour, with short obtuse rays : panicle dense: ovate : level-topped : radical leaves, oblong: acute : arrowshaped : entire, with obtuse lobes.

Scurvy-grass, or *cochlearia Grœnlandica,* is found here, as in all northern countries, in great plenty. The root of this herb is white, rather thick, elongated, covered with hairy fibres : the whole herb is smooth, somewhat fleshy, very various in size : *stems* leafy, angular, branched in a corymbose manner. Flowers white : calyx obtuse : spreading : concave : petals inversely egg-shaped : entire : silicles globular : slightly veined : crowned with a short style : seeds, five or six in a shell. It has a warm and bitter taste; a pungent, rather unpleasant smell, when bruised. Its active matter is extracted by maceration in proof spirit, and is said to be of great use in scurvy; but of this I have had no experience.

Chick-weed is very common, and belongs to the species *arenaria luterifloria,* or side-flowing sand-wort. The leaves are ovate : obtuse : peduncles lateral : two-flowered. The stem is short, small, simple : leaves smooth, on short footstalks : peduncles single : long: bifid: axillary : corolla larger than the calyx.

I found a considerable number of auriculas in the glen near the factory; they appeared to belong to the species of *primula corturoides.* The leaves are of a fine green colour, without any mealiness; variously lobed, and toothed: flowers purple, and very handsome.

There is also an herb, called by the Indians jackasheypuk, found here, though rather in sparing quantity. It much resembles creeping-box; and is only used by the English, or Indians, to mix with tobacco, which makes it smoke mild and pleasant.

During these excursions we were a good deal annoyed with the musquitos, having neglected to provide ourselves with any means of defence against their troublesome bites. These insects are of the gnat tribe, and subsist on the blood and juices of larger animals, which they suck by means of their proboscis. In the larva state they live in stagnant waters. They have a small respiratory tube near the tail, and the head armed with hooks, by means of which they seize upon and secure their prey. The pupa is incurvated and subovate, with respiratory tubes near the head. They appear to belong to the species *culex pipiens*, being cinereous with eight brown rings; the antennæ of the male are pectinated. They abound principally in the neighbourhood of marshes, low grounds, and stagnant water. Wherever they fix their sting a little tumour or pustule usually arises. The disagreeable itching which this excites is most effectually allayed by the application of volatile alkali ; the application of cold water also affords relief.

The auroræ borealis are not only singularly beautiful in their appearance, but afford to travellers, by their almost constant effulgence, a very beautiful light during the entire night; sometimes, indeed, it diffuses a variegated splendour, which is not inferior to that of the full-moon. They generally stretch from north-east to north-west, and are much fainter in the former quarter. In its appearance it resembles electrical light when viewed in a vacuum. They always commence like a mist, on the northern part of the horizon, which is then clearer towards the west. This thickness of the air commonly arranges itself in the form of the segment of a circle. The point of its circumference that is visible soon acquires a border of a whiteish light, which gradually increases, and from whence proceeds one or several luminous arches. At this period the darting of the coloured rays commences, some from the segment of a circle, and others from the arch itself; by their motion, the space which they bear always seems open, and their appearances increase in motion and vividness of colour, with a proportionate augmentation of the whole meteor. The various coruscations cause an appearance of great confusion, and it occasionally seems to vanish in part, speedily re-appearing with increased splendour.* They are frequently accompanied with a rustling or whizzing kind of noise. This I have never heard, but have been informed of the fact by persons who have resided many years in the country.

Many attempts have been made to assign the immediate cause of this phenomenon. Ever since the identity of lightning, and of the electric matter, has been ascertained, philosophers have been naturally led to look for the explication of aerial meteors in the principles of electricity, and there is now, I believe, but little doubt that most of them, but particularly

---

* I have frequently hung a thermometer on deck while the light was most intense, but could not observe that there was any elevation whatever produced.

that of which we have been speaking, depends upon these principles. Dr. Hamilton, of this city, was, it seems, the first who attempted to discover any positive evidence of the electrical nature of the aurora borealis. The only proof, however, which he advances is an experiment of Hawkesbier, by which the electrical fluid is shown to assume appearances resembling the aurora borealis, when it passes through a vacuum. He observed, that when the air was most perfectly exhausted the streams of electrical matter were then quite white; but when a small quantity of air was let in, the light assumed more of a purple colour. The flashing of the light, therefore, from the dense region of the atmosphere into such as are more rare, and the transition through mediums of different densities, he considers as the cause of the aurora, and of the different colours it assumes. Dr. Halley, and, more lately, Mr. Dalton, have advanced many ingenious arguments in favour of the opinion that this phenomenon depends on the quantity of magnetic fluid existing in the atmosphere, the polarity of magnets having been observed to be disturbed during its appearance. It has been proved, however, particularly by Perecotte, that this disturbance does not always take place on such occasions; and, as the same circumstance is observed to happen when the atmosphere is in a positive state of electricity, the theory itself becomes highly questionable. Whatever may be the immediate cause of this phenomenon, it is evidently connected with the condensation of vapour from the air, as, during their appearance, there always is observed a copious deposition of dew, or hoar-frost. Hence, perhaps, this meteor* is so common in those latitudes where the vericular vapour hangs near to the earth's surface, and when its evaporation and precipitation are slowly taking place.

The halos which occasionally surround the sun and moon deserve to be next considered. This appearance occurs only when there is a slight fog in the atmosphere. They rarely accompany the sun, owing to these vapours being so readily dissipated by the calorific rays of that planet. This phenomenon appears to be occasioned by the rays of light striking against a cloud, or body of vapour, which, although considerably uniform and dense, is still so rare as to allow them to be scattered at the point of incidence, and which are thus reflected and refracted,

---

* See, on this subject, Robertson's History of the Atmosphere.—Dr. Halley's Philosophical Transactions, No. 347, p. 406.—Kirwan's Transactions of the Royal Irish Academy, 1778, p. 80.—Franklin's Experiments and Observations, 1769, p. 49.—Philosophical Transactions, Vol. xlviii. Part 1. p. 358. —Priestly's History of Electricity.

from every point around giving the appearance of a luminous circle. An appearance, not unlike this, may sometimes be observed round the lights in the streets during damp weather; or, by rubbing the eyes also, a similar appearance may be observed, owing to the refraction of the rays of light as they reach the eyes, by the contents of the carunculæ lachrymales and glands of the eye-lids, which, owing to the pressure, are spread over the surface of the cornea.

In these remote latitudes the stars are said to twinkle with a fiery redness; but this I did not observe. The cone of red light which is observed to accompany the rising and setting of the sun, in this and other northern countries, is probably owing to the great quantity of vericular vapour with which the lower parts of the atmosphere are always loaded in these climates.

Vocabulary of the Dialects.

I shall here give a few words of Northern and Chippeway Indian language, which I wrote down during my stay at Fort York, beginning with that of the Oochepayyans, or northern Indians. I am principally indebted to Mr. Swaine, one of the inland governors, to whom I take this opportunity of returning many thanks for the kind and polite attention which I received from him while at York Fort.

I - - - -	Nitha.	Ye - - - -	Kithawow.
Thou - - -	Kihta.	He, or she - -	Witha.
We - - -	Withawow.	You and I - -	Kithanow.
They - - -	Nithanan.		

A knife - - - -	Muk a man.
A fork - - - -	Chas chas chip muin.
A hog - - - -	Koo koos.
A fire - - - -	Ukastaoo.
A house - - - -	Has has heguin.
Bread - - -	Herakanou.
A duck - - -	Sheeship.
A goose - - -	Nischow.
A swan - - -	Wap a say.
Give me - - -	Pich assummin.
A coat - - - -	Shutagan.
A shoe - - -	Muskasin.
A hat - - -	Stutan.
Hair - - -	Piiyy.
A kettle - - -	Arkik.
A pot - - -	Minniguaggan.
A hand - - -	Michichi.
A man - - -	Mapin.
A woman - - -	Huskow.
A small canoe - -	Wossquichiman.
A ship - - - -	Quassatik.
A star - - - -	Achak.
An evil spirit - -	Willikoo.
A pipe - - -	Oospoggan.
A piece of stick -	Mistik.
A handkerchief -	Tapastaggan.
A pair of stockings -	Ootassa.
A watch - -	Pisumakan.
A porcupine - -	Kaquaw.
A beaver - -	Amisk.
A buffaloe - -	Mistus.
A dog - - -	Atim.

A horse	- - -	Mistatam.
Paint	- - -	Oothuman.
A bow	- - -	Achapi.
An arrow	- - -	Akusk.
A gun	- - -	Paskisaggan.
A hatchet	- - -	Chikahaggan.
A trout	- - -	Mamakus.
A sturgeon	- - -	Hamaoo.
Feathers	- - -	Oopaawaoo.
A rope	- - -	Pinriniquan.
A paddle	- - -	Upowoi.
A deer	- - -	Atik.
A wolf	- - -	Managan.
A leg	- - -	Uskat.
A foot	- - -	Hoossit.
A candle	- - -	Wasasuskatoonamaooin.
A box	- - -	Mislikooit.
A key	- - -	Apilukahagin.
Flesh	- - -	Wiaash.
A snow shoe	- - -	Kithanowweasamak.
The Supreme Being	- -	Kisshamanatou.
A pair of snuffers	- -	Kikisouhaggan.
A window	- - -	Wassanamouin.
A tree growing	- -	Mistikgahchimmussoot.
The bark of a tree	- -	Wetthakeisk.
A musquitoe	- - -	Luggimaoo.
A sand-fly	- - -	Pikoos.
A bull-dog	- - -	Mississak.
A frog	- - -	Atheek.
A toad	- - -	Pippikootalayoo.
A day sun	- - -	Kishikowapissim.
A night sun	- - -	Tibbiskowapissim.
A fox	- - -	Makashis.
An otter	- - -	Nukik.
A martin	- - -	Wapastan.
A bear	- - -	Musquah.
A white bear	- - -	Mahpusk.
A mink	- - -	Shaquasshoo.
An ermin	- - -	Sikus.
A skunk	- - -	Sikak.
A badger	- - -	Mistamusk.
A squirrel	- - -	Anikoochus.
A squirrel	- - -	Sassakawappiskoos.
An owl	- - -	Ohoo.
A partridge	- - -	Pethayoo.
A plover	- - -	Pusscoochussin.

A mouse	-	-	- Appacoosish.
Brandy -	-	-	- Iscootawahpoi.
Powder	-	-	- Kusketayoo.
A gun -	-	-	- Parkissceggan.
A flint -	-	-	- Chakasahuggan.
A steel -	-	-	- Apeth.
A ramrod	-	-	- Cikuchiskkahaganatik.
The wind	-	-	- Thutin.
Tobacco	-	-	- Chisthamon.
The nose	-	-	- Oocoo.
The mouth	-	-	- Ootoon.
The chin	-	-	- Wasquineyoo.
A tooth	-	-	- Oowipit.
The ear	-	-	- Ootawaki.
The eye	-	-	- Ooskishik.
The cheeks	-	-	- Oowanawè.
Countryman -	-	-	- Tootamuk.
Northern lights	-	-	- Chipaak.
Thunder	-	-	- Pithashoouck.
Lightning	-	-	- Wasusquitaoo.
Snow -	-	-	- Koona.
Cold -	-	-	- Kishinou.
Ice -	-	-	- Miskoome.
A very cold day	-	-	- Naspichkishanou.
One -	-	-	- Piak.
Two -	-	-	- Nishoo.
Three -	-	-	- Nistoo.
Four -	-	-	- Naoo.
Five -	-	-	- Naanin.
Six -	-	-	- Ootwasik.
Seven -	-	-	- Niswassik.
Eight -	-	-	- Swasik.
Nine -	-	-	- Sak.
Ten -	-	-	- Mitath.
A lark -	-	-	- Makawk.
The ground -	-	-	- Uski.
A tent -	-	-	- Migoapek.
A shirt	-	-	- Pukayanasagas.
A lock	-	-	- Alhuppissaik.
The arm	-	-	- Uspittooin.
The thigh -	-	-	- Pawom.
Good -	-	-	- Mithawashin.
Bad -	-	-	- Mathatin.
A stone	-	-	- Asini.
A book, or any thing written			Misanahagan.
A spy-glass -	-	-	- Oothahpahchiggun.

A few familiar Phrases in the Chippeway Language.

I may here remark, that this is one of the mother-tongues of North America, and is usually spoken among the chiefs, who reside about the great lakes, as far south as the Ohio, and as far north as Hudson's Bay.

How do you do, friend? - -	Way way nee jee?
In good health, I thank you. -	Meegwotch nobum pemurtus.
What news? - - - - - -	Tarnin mergunxmegal?
I have none. - - - - - -	Caú ween arwayyor.
Have you had a good hunt this winter? - - - - - -	Nishisghin geosay nogome bebóne?
Yes, a very good hunt. - -	Angaymer o hisshishin.
What lake did you hunt at last winter? - - - - - -	Hawwaneeyawassakiegan kee geosay?
At the skunk lake. - - - -	Sheekark sakiegan.
What is there at that lake? -	Waygonin woity ha sakiegan.
Beaver, but not much. - -	Amik cawween gwotch.
This is English. - - - -	Maunder saggonash.
Let us eat. - - - - - -	Hawwissinnimin.
It is very good. - - - - -	Hunjeyta o hishshishin.
Sit down. - - - - - -	Mantetappy.
I want to smoke a pipe. - -	Nee wee suggersoy.
I will go. - - - - - -	Nin gamarcha.
That is right. - - - - -	Neegwoyack.
Not yet. - - - - - - -	Kamarchy.
How many beaver-skins will you take for this? - - -	Andersoy appiminiquy keetarpenan mor?
Twenty. - - - - - - -	Neesh tanner.
Take them, friend. - - -	Tarpenan, neecarnis.
Your health, friend. - - -	Kee tallenemanco.
I love you. - - - - - -	Neezargaykeen.
I am well. - - - - - -	Pemartissey nin.
I am dry. - - - - - -	Sparchlay nin.
I am hungry. - - - - -	Bocketty nin.
I am cold. - - - - - -	Geessennar nin.
I am lazy. - - - - - -	Kittinnin.
I will go to bed. - - - -	Peshemo hin gamarchar.
Get up, friend. - - - -	Genishear, neegee.
Take courage. Farewell, friend. - - - - - -	Haguarmissey, way, waynegee.

VOYAGE

TO THE

NORTH POLE,

IN THE FRIGATE THE SYRENE;

INCLUDING

A PHYSICAL AND GEOGRAPHICAL NOTICE

RELATIVE TO

THE ISLAND OF ICELAND.

BY THE

CHEVALIER DE LA POIX DE FREMINVILLE,

LIEUTENANT, CHIEF OF THE BRIGADE OF THE MARINE CADETS, AND A
MEMBER OF SEVERAL LEARNED SOCIETIES.

LONDON:

PRINTED FOR SIR RICHARD PHILLIPS AND Co.
BRIDE-COURT, BRIDGE-STREET.

1819.

THE CHEVALIER DE FREMINVILLE

TO THE EDITOR.

—

Brest, June 19, 1819.

AT a time when the Literati of Europe are waiting with anxiety the result of the new expedition which the English government have sent to explore the passage to the North Pole, and to resolve the problem whether Greenland be an island; it may be presumed that a brief relation of a Voyage to the North Sea, in 1806, performed by some officers of the French marine, of whom I was one, will prove acceptable and interesting.

This expedition, after encountering a number of difficulties, penetrated to latitude 80°; and it will be observed, that the attempt made by the English last year could only penetrate those seas to the latitude of 80° 32″. In the course of our voyage, the various interesting incidents that occurred, particularly at the Island of Iceland, will render this brief narrative, I venture to affirm, not only worthy of observation, but highly interesting.

VOYAGE

NORTH POLE.

=

Relation of a Voyage made to the North Pole, in the Frigate the Syrene; including a Physical and Geographical Notice relative to the Island of Iceland. By the CHE-VALIER DE LA POIX DE FREMINVILLE, *Lieutenant, Chief of the Brigade of the Company of the Marine Cadets, and a Member of several learned Societies.*

SINCE the time of Duguay Trouin, the French government had not turned its attention to the North Seas. In the course of the last war, an expedition to these seas was projected, for the purpose of annoying the whale-fishery carried on there by the English, and to take and destroy the vast fleets that are annually employed by them in this trade. Such a scheme was pregnant with much danger; nevertheless, the advantages likely to result from it were great in more relations than one. Government, therefore, now resolved to put the plan in practice; and, in consequence, three frigates were armed. The command of the squadron was confided to Captain le Duc, an experienced seaman, who had already made several voyages in the Hyperborean Ocean.

A resolution was taken to collect every possible advantage from an expedition that should advance as near as possible to the pole, to penetrate into seas almost hitherto unexplored; military operations were not to be the only object; the sciences were to come in for a share of the probable benefits. Captain le Duc, in his instructions, was directed to let slip no opportunity to avail himself of any astronomical and geographical observations and facts that might conduce to the improvement of our hydrography, to this day very imperfect, with respect to the North Seas.

The minister of marine determined that an officer should embark, as supplementary, in the frigate the Syrene, wherein the commodore sailed, to superintend, in an especial manner, the hydrographic labours. I was selected for this undertaking; a better choice might doubtless have been made; but

well knowing how to value a distinction of this honourable
kind, I can with truth affirm, that our scientific operations,
during the voyage, are entitled to a measure of public confidence. On our return, our papers were submitted to the in-
spection of the illustrious Bougainville; and this prince of
French navigators was pleased to sanction them with his ap-
probation.

The division, or squadron, consisting of the frigates the
Syrene, the Guerière, and the Revanche, put to sea on the
28th of March, 1806. After frequent calms for a number of
days together, in the gulph of Gascony, a very violent gale
dispersed them, and obliged the Syrene to make for the Azore
Islands, which had been fixed upon as the first point of rendezvous in case of separation.

After cruising two days within view of the isles of Corvo
and Flores, the squadron again got together, and immediately
bore away in a northerly direction.

We were not long before we felt the effects of a piercing
cold, which gave us reason to regret the mild temperature of
the Azores. Continual foul weather, which did not allow us
for fifteen days to sail, except with lowered topsails, led the
captain to conceive, that as the rigorous season was likely to
be of longer continuance than usual, it was too soon to attempt a passage into the frigid zone; in consequence of this,
he determined to cruise about ten or twelve days in the latitude of Cape Farewell, on the coast of Greenland.

Our course, in coming from the Azores to these latitudes,
had passed over the points wherein a number of doubtful spots
are marked on the great chart of the Atlantic Ocean, published in 1786; and which, perhaps, have no existence, or only
form the little island of Jaquet, inaccurately fixed by the
voyagers to Newfoundland; their reports, it is certain, have
often obtained more credit than they were entitled to.

We steered for ten days on the parallel of 59 deg. 30 min.
but having to encounter very rough gales of a northerly wind,
all our endeavours to keep longer in that bearing were fruitless. Being obliged to keep close to the Cape, we were driven
back to the south, as far as the 58th parallel. To make some
advantage of a circumstance so contrary, we beat about for
the Isle of Bas, or Wrisland, placed in the chart of M. de
Verdun in 58 deg. 11 min. lat. N. and in 28 deg. 13 min. lon.
W. This islet, which was nothing but an extinguished volcano, had become a rendezvous for the Greenland fishermen
who first discovered it; the Dutch had formed some establish-
ments on it, for the preparation of whale-oil, but it disappeared about sixty years ago, and has never since been

noticed. It is conceived, that, like many other volcanic islets, it has been swallowed up by some submarine convulsion, examples of the like having frequently occurred.

Reaching the point assigned to the Isle of Bas, in the chart above cited, we could trace no vestige of it; but as we had a rough sea, with short and rippling waves, we judged we might be over the spot it once occupied. We sounded for better assurance, but a line of 200 fathoms could find no bottom. Such submarine phenomena, doubtless the most extraordinary of any that volcanic eruptions produce, are frequent in the Northern Ocean, at least in the tracks occupied by the long volcanic chain that stretches from the 58th to the 72d degree of latitude. This chain commences to the north of Scotland; and the basaltic archipelagos of the Hebrides, of the Orkneys, and Shetland Isles, form the first rings of it. Stretching afterwards to the N. W. across the oceanic whirlpools, it appears again at the Ferro Islands, then at Iceland, the most extensive theatre of ignivomous eruptions to be found on the surface of our globe. From Iceland, the chain goes on to join the Isle of Jean Mayen, or Trinity, where it appears to end, after traversing under water a space of more than 260 marine leagues. In advancing more to the north, we find nothing in the character of the lands that presents features of a volcanic soil; Bear's Island, and Spitzberg, are wholly calcareous.

The weather now becoming milder, we bore away for the north; and in a few days we had sight of the coasts of Iceland. Their dark profile delineated a rough sketch of its steep, rocky, indented shores, on a misty horizon; in the N. W. at a very considerable distance, appeared an enormous mountain, which we judged might be Mount Hecla; but the bad weather, for three days successively, not admitting of any astronomical observations, I will not affirm that it was actually that famous volcano, which had now been in a tranquil state the twelve preceding years.

We made sail for the north-east, coasting the land, but at a considerable distance; the weather cleared up, during the short night which succeeded to the day of our seeing land, and a pure serene sky on the day ensuing brought to view, on another point of the coast, a *jokul*, or mountain, of a prodigious height, entirely covered with snow; its summit, which reached far above the clouds, reflected the rays of the rising sun, which tinging it with a beautiful rose-colour, blended insensibly with the whiteness of its flanks, and produced an admirable effect. Our observations enabled us to ascertain this mountain for the jocul of Knapafells, on the point of Wester, to the S. E. of the island.

Being thus assured of our position, we bore away at large, keeping always to the E. N. E. We were in the track wherein the maps generally place the Isle of Enckuysen, the existence of which was, nevertheless, considered as very doubtful. In our course we must have passed directly over the point wherein the chart of Bellin places it. As the problem of its existence was a matter of some interest to resolve, and we could effect it without going out of our course, we stationed some of our company on the look-out.

At night-fall some of the men gave notice of a shoal, or ridge, a-head; in fact, the sea, at a little distance in front, seemed to us covered with thousands of birds, of the kind of petrels and seagulls, the vast numbers of which, from their white plumage, resembled at a distance the froth of waves rippling over breakers; we went about a mile to windward of the pretended shoal, and discovered it to be the floating and half putrid carcase of a dead whale, thus serving for food to an immense multitude of sea-fowl.

Next day, May 12, we discovered land; it was, in reality, the Isle of Enckuysen, to the N. N. W. of us, at the distance of about two leagues and a half. We fixed the position of its southerly point at 64 deg. 54 min. lat. and 12 deg. 48 min. long. W.

The Isle of Enckuysen, generally placed in the charts much too westerly of its real situation, and too near the coast of Iceland, appeared to us to be about four leagues in extent, in the direction of N. N. E. to S. S. W.; it has just elevation enough not to render the approach dangerous.

May 14th, we crossed the Arctic polar circle at 10 deg. 14 min. long. W.

May 17th. In the latitude of 72 deg. we noticed, with surprize, the first floating ice; it was unusual for the season to meet with ice so early; it is usually to be found about the middle of May, but only in from 76 to 80 degrees of latitude. Captain Phipps sent, in 1773, from England, to explore the passage of the Pole, could see no ice till he had reached the N. W. part of the coast of Spitzberg.

Next day we came abreast of a very large island of floating ice, with fleaks of prodigious dimensions; these masses, doubtless detached from the immense banks that surround the Spitzberg, from the diversity of their shapes, and their curious infractions and indentations, presented a spectacle altogether unique for most of our company. Their friction produced a stunning kind of noise, like that which the sea-water makes over a strand of pebbles and gravel.

We cleared those mountains of ice-flakes, many of which rose to the height of our main-top-mast; they were transparent, and of a most beautiful azure blue.

Still bearing on to the N. E. we endeavoured to near Beering Island *(Beereh Eylandt,)* situated in 74 deg. 33 min. lat. Its extent is not above four or five leagues. It is reported that the Russians have discovered in it a very rich silver mine.

May 19th, at midnight, (there was no darkness then during the night) a bluish lustre, visible in the horizon, warned us of the approach of the ice. This phenomenon, produced by the refraction of the rays of light on the water, is a sure sign of the proximity of considerable bergs ; in fact, we observed one soon after, but consisting of blocks so large and so close together, that there appeared no interval through which we could penetrate. We coasted along it for several hours; it was covered with thousands of *phocæ*, that is, seals, or sea-calves *(phoca vitulina,* L.) that were rolling about, and seemed to be sporting in the snow. We were so near that we could salute them with discharges of our musketry, but were unable to kill any, as the balls merely slid over their hard smooth skin without piercing it. Knowing that they were dispatched at once with a blow on the nose, we prepared a boat and descended, to the number of seven or eight, among immense heaps, the smallest of which were five feet in length. Our presence did not terrify them, and they viewed us with a stupid kind of stare. We knocked some of them on the head with our oars, when they tried to make their escape, uttering a noise like the shrill barking of a young dog.

It is generally thought that seals derive the faculty which they possess of staying long under water, to the botal aperture, which they preserve during life.* I wished to inform myself on this important point of comparative anatomy, and took care to open the heart of one of those we had taken ; I found the notion to be erroneous, that the botal aperture was entirely closed, and that, of course, the blood could not pass from the veins into the arterial system without previously crossing the lungs ; then to disengage itself by the contact of the external air from the carbone which it contains. It is evident, therefore, that although seals may plunge under water for a consi-

---

* In hot-blooded animals, the botal aperture is only to be found in the fœtus, and becomes extinct instantly after the birth.

derable time, respiration is as necessary to promote the circulation of their blood as it is in other mammiferous animals; neither can they dispense with the necessity of coming up to the surface of the water, from time to time, to take
breath.

I found the stomach of my seal filled with intestinal worms
alive, that appeared to me to belong to the genus of *echinor-
hyncs.*

In proceeding along the borders of the ice, we found it
stretching along to the east, after having obliged us to mount
up to 75 deg. 28 min. and having, in course, passed by
the latitude of Beering Island, the pursuit of which we now
discontinued.

May 22d, a profound calm surprized us, in sight of an island
of ice of considerable length and extent. As long as the calm
lasted we were hemmed round with a groupe of cetaceous animals, from twenty-five to thirty feet in length, marked as the
genus *Delphinus,* by Linnæus, but which, I conceive, ought
to constitute a new species. I have already published a description of them, with cuts, in the Bulletin of Sciences of
the Philomathic Society, under the name of *Delphinus Coro-
natus,* or the Crowned Dolphin ; this epithet comes from two
concentric circles, of a yellow colour, that these animals have
on the crown of the head.

A breeze springing up in the night, we were drawing nearer
to the islet of ice that stood to the north of us; we tried to
find an opening or passage, but none appeared; and after
coasting it a long time, keeping to the east, we perceived it
ready to join another considerable mass, and that the interval
between them was so narrow and so perplexed with floating
flakes and heaps of ice, that a passage was impracticable. We
tacked about with an intention to double its western extremity,
which we could not accomplish till next day.

After clearing it we bore to the north-east, falling straight
in with the south Cape of Spitzberg, which we were in hopes
of soon reaching; but in this we were disappointed, as another
island of ice came to present new obstacles. On the eastern
side of it we could perceive an opening or avenue ; we plunged
into it, but scarcely had we entered, when a thick fog came
over us and obliged us to exert particular care to avoid striking against some of the large floating fragments of ice that
surrounded us.

The fog lasted two hours; when, clearing up, we could see
the ice behind us closing up so as to intercept our return.
We were now ingulphed on every side, immured as in a kind
of basin that might be about two leagues in extent. This, to

us, was a situation truly alarming; we tacked about in every direction in quest of an outlet; one only was visible; but the floating fragments that blocked it up made the attempt to be, at first, considered as impracticable. At length our commandant, finding the icy-basin that shut us in was condensing and accumulating, decided that we had no time to lose, or hesitate between the certainty of being quickly locked in the ice and a solitary chance of escape. We made all sail then to get through this perilous streight; and, after running the risk a hundred times of being dashed against the floating shoals that were thickening around us, we were fortunate enough to clear the passage with the loss only of some sheets of our copper, that were carried away by icy morsels we had to bear up against.

May 31st, we discovered the land of Spitzberg; at a very great distance we could trace the South Cape, which stood N.N.E. as also Hope Island, which lies a little more to the east, at a short distance. A solid plain of impenetrable ice prevented our getting near it, and, being obliged to stretch along it in a run to the north-west, we soon lost sight of that dreary shore.

June 3d, a deep inlet was visible in the middle of the immense islets of ice that we were coasting along; we entered into it, and had a toilsome passage of about twelve hours; but it was so blocked up, that we were obliged at last to return. A heavy gale from the S. W. bringing vast masses of icy fragments into contact, threatened to close in upon us, and it was not without prodigious exertions that we got at length into the open sea.

We now began to lose all hopes of reaching Spitzberg, which was one part of our destination. Some days before we had captured some whale-ships, the captains of which assured us that they had been engaged in the same fruitless attempt, and that the ice had rendered all approach impracticable.

Our ships' companies were very much worn down with incessant fatigue, in a painful navigation, that called for constant watching and active exertion. The scurvy was preying upon us, and some of our best seamen had fallen victims to it; our water and wood grew scanty; the want of wood prevented us from getting at water with the melted ice. We tried, but in vain, to procure heat enough for this purpose, by resorting to different methods in all the warmest parts of the ship.

The perplexities of such a situation called for a speedy change of measures; our chief, however, to shelter himself from every imputation of neglect, would make one more ef-

fort to find a passage through the solid ice, advancing as far
north as possible; in this hope, we kept continually bearing
up along the chain of immoveable ice that stretched to the
N. W.

In fact, we reached the 80th degree of latitude, without
gaining any inlet or opening. The whole vast plain, or rather
continent of ice, lies in a direction to the west. We coasted
it for several days without finding any break or interruption,
and I am convinced that it joins all along to the ice that borders the coast of Greenland.

I shall not attempt to describe the impressions that the solitary and dreary aspect of this icy continent produced on our
minds. Its situation on the limits of our globe, the profound
silence pervading its vast domain, the total absence of animal
life—every thing seemed to exhibit an image of death, and of
all nature in mourning. The gloomy spectacle was not,
however, without a sort of peculiar attraction; masses of ice,
illumined in different modes, reflecting the light in a thousand
different ways, from the odd assemblage of their needle points
or ends; their fractures, their varied shapes, presented views
as uncommon as they were astonishing. We used frequently to
compare them to the ruins of some most extensive capital dis-
cerned at a distance; the imagination taking wing, would de-
pict colonnades, towers, steeples, castles, fortresses, &c. In the
remote back-ground appeared a chain of lofty mountains of ice
that terminated the horizon.

There being no prospect of penetrating further north, and
it being impossible to touch at Spitzberg, we resolved on
steering southward, having taken and burnt, in the north
seas, fifteen whale-fishery ships.

Here we may remark, that Captain Phipps did not encounter the chain of ice till he was north of Spitzberg, whereas it
blocked up our passage at the 77th degree.

In the course of our navigation in these parts, we never had
a heavy sea, though the wind was frequently very high; the
waves were, in some measure, fettered under the mass of ice.
We could observe, however, after Captain Phipps, on nearing
the great banks, even in calm weather, big surges coming
gently from the south.

In those high latitudes the sky is seldom so clear as to be
able to make astronomical observations. We availed ourselves
of every favourable circumstance that occurred, but it was
only three times that we could take the meridian altitude of
the sun at midnight.

Scarcity and scorbutic diseases called for prompt relief;

our commandant at first was making for the Bay of Strunsa, in Danish Lapland; but contrary winds forced us to relinquish this intention, and to bear away for Iceland.

July 3d, we were off Langeness, the N.E. point of that large island; as we meant to bring up in the Bay of Patrix Fiord, at the opposite extremity, our course made us nearly go the circuit of it, and we seized the opportunity of adding to our geographical information, with respect to the coasts of a country so little known.

Langeness, or Long Point, is easily to be distinguished; it is a low land, stretching a great way into the sea. I take it to be the only part of the island that has so very little of elevation; all the coasts are lofty, abrupt, and perpendicularly steep. Scarcely had we doubled this point, when we found high lands over-hanging us like walls; their rough and craggy indentations, the basaltic columns of their brown sides, feasted the eye with a spectacle truly picturesque; but not a glimpse of verdure, no signs of vegetation were discernible on a soil of which Vulcan alone seems to have possessed the property. At a very great distance we could distinguish the smoking summit of Mount Krafte, a considerable volcano, that makes part of the mountainous chain in the N.E. of the island.

On the 5th, we discovered the small island of Walzback, distant about five leagues from the Terra Firma; it stands so low, that it scarcely appears above the level of the sea. Kergueleu, who was in these seas in the years 1767 and 1768, reports, from the evidence of the whale-fishers, that no passage existed between Walsback and Iceland, from a chain of breakers stretching through it. We determined to ascertain this point, and bore up into the passage, finding a considerable depth of water everywhere, as it is all along on the coast. We were continually sounding, and the lead always brought up a portion of heavy volcanic sand, or a kind of black puzzolane.

July 6th, we reached the Isles of Portland, at the most southern extremity of the island; it was at this point that the Marquis Verdun de la Crenne terminated his voyage of discovery; when he came to visit Iceland, in 1771, in the frigate La Flore, having with him Borda and Pingré, for scientific purposes. The labours of those valuable men well deserve the praise of rigid accuracy; we have observed that the chart published by them in 1776, with respect to all the parts of the coast of Iceland which they visited, that is to say, the part from the Isles of Portland to Patrix Fiord, is traced with a precision that leaves nothing to be wished for, either in point of positions or of configurations.

We owe also a just tribute of eulogium to the engravings of the views of the coasts annexed to the relation of the voyage of La Flore, and designed by Ozanne, employed on board our frigate; nothing can be more correct, even to the very smallest details. As to the views of the same portions of coast, engraved in the relation of Kerguelen, they are rather to be censured than commended.

After exploring the whole southern coast of Iceland, we passed between Cape Reikia-ness and the Rocks of the Birds, in Icelandish, Ryke-yse. It was here that a very singular submarine phenomenon occurred, in 1783; the sea appeared covered with a light-bluish flame, through an extent of more than a mile; it lasted several hours, and occasioned a very great consternation among the inhabitants of the neighbouring coast. When the flame ceased, a small island appeared on the scite, the surface of which was covered with pumice-stones and volcanic ashes. This islet has since disappeared, probably by another convulsion of the same kind.

In proceeding northwards, we crossed the great gulph of Faxa Fiordur,* having a view of Mount Jengel, or the Jokul of the west; its top covered with snow, though at more than twenty leagues distance. This is taken to be the highest mountain in Iceland.

It was in the gulph of Faxa Fiordur that we saw the sea covered with a sort of mollusca, or rather of *radiaire*, that seemed to constitute a new genus affiliated with the *medusas* and the *beroes*. I gave it the name of idya; a description, with a plate of it, was published in the Bulletin of Sciences, under the name of *idya Islandica*.

After doubling the Cape and Mount Jengel, we crossed the gulph of Breyde Fiordur; and, on the 13th of July, we entered the Bay of Patrix Fiord, where we anchored in eleven fathoms water, near the Danish factory.

The Bay of Patrix Fiord lies in 65 deg. 35 min. 45 sec. N. lat. and 26 deg. 29 min. 53 sec. W. long.; like all the other bays of the island, it is very deep, and encompassed with lofty, abrupt mountains. The entrance to it is very easy, and there is no danger to be apprehended.

The Danish factory stands on a low point, consisting of ancient lavas; the anchorage is within the point. The Danish establishment is divided into three wooden houses, one of which serves as a dwelling for the director, and the others are warehouses. Round about lie scattered the wretched huts of

---

* In Icelandish, the word *fiord*, or *fiordur*, signifies a gulph, or bay; *jokul*, or *jockel*, is appropriated to the high mountains.

the poor Icelanders, half buried in earth ; the roofing only, made of whales' ribs, rises above the surface. Behind these is a pool of fresh water, which has given to Patrix Fiord the Icelandish name of *Vatneyre*, the Water Town.

The bay may be about three leagues in length, from W. to E. ; its greatest breadth is about a league and a half. Very near the middle is a large sand-bank, which gets dry at low-water, and over which large vessels cannot pass. Besides the town or village of Vatneyre, there are others dispersed about the bay, at certain distances ; the most considerable is that of Sadlangsdaler, where there is a Lutheran church; it lies on the side opposite to the Danish factory, on the banks of a sheet of water well stocked with salmon.

A chart of all the parts of the island that we visited, with a number of our own new discoveries and original remarks, were transmitted, on our return, to the minister of marine, together with a collection of seventeen designs, representing views of different coasts, some tracts or situations in Iceland, and various objects of natural history, either new or but little known.

The country round the bay presents a gloomy sort of prospect, but dignified and imposing ; every thing bears the impression of volcanic convulsions and of the ravages of earthquakes. All the mountains seem, at it were, calcinated ; you cannot walk except over lava and basalt, the fragments of which, disjoined, roll under your steps with a rattling and stunning noise ; only two colours, red and black, diversify the lugubrious landscape within the circle of your view. A good scene-painter for a theatre, who would make a drawing of the infernal regions, could copy no better model than one of the situations of Iceland.

One of the oddest spectacles that I ever beheld, was a very extensive platform, serving as a *cimex*, or crown, to the mountain that overlooks the anchorage of Vatneyre. It is composed of large tables of basalt, from eight to ten feet of surface, but on a level, and arranged regularly, one beside another, like so many leaves in a book ; the edge, not above four inches in thickness, every where meeting your view. In some parts, these basaltic tables, overset by earthquakes, yield such an image of disorder and confusion, that you would be led to think the spot (whereon no sign of vegetation or life appears) to be made up of the ruins of the globe.

In low places, at the entrance of the valleys, there is some little appearance of verdure ; a thick turf, with a few flowers scattered on it, may be seen on the banks of the running waters. I collected a number of plants, but little known in.

Europe, large enough to form nearly the whole of the Islandic Flora.

Not a single tree is to be seen in the whole district of Patrix Fiord; and even in the other parts of the island, it is with difficulty you can light on a few dwarfish willows, and some stunted birch-trees. Many fruitless attempts have been made to sow or plant the pine and fir, from Europe; but though they have succeeded in the fine season, the young shoots were never able to stand the long and rigorous winter of a climate so frozen. No credit must be given to what M. Horrebow reports, in his description of Iceland, wherein he makes mention of fruitful plains, and immense pastures; his work, drawn up from the false accounts of the Dutch fishermen, is replete with the grossest errors. That of Anderson, built on the same authorities, is but little better; and the fact is, that we have in Europe but very lame and imperfect accounts of this country, so very extraordinary and interesting in many respects.

Iceland extends from N. to S. between 66 deg. 44 min. and 62 deg. 22 min. 30 sec. lat. and from W. to E. between 27 deg. 5 min. and 18 deg. 26 min. long. W. of the meridian of Paris. Its greatest length may be about 133 leagues, and its breadth about fifty-six; the island contains a superficies of about 5,500 square leagues.

Exclusive of a number of towns and hamlets, there are four principal cities; but in Europe, these cities would only pass for villages; they are built of wood, with planks brought from Denmark. The first is Holum, in the north; the second, named Skalholt, is in the south; both are the sees of a bishop. The third lies to the S. W., and is called Bessested; this is the residence of the governor, and the only place in the island where there is a small fort armed with six eight-pounders, mounted on carriages that are falling to pieces with age; to the N. E. is the fourth city, called Skrida.

The interior of Iceland is but little known; the whole island, however, may be pronounced a mass of volcanic rocks, whose sides, black and burnt, whose summits, sharp and craggy, present a prospect of the most singular kind. There is not a single point in this sad country which does not seem to have undergone the action of fire; one consequence is, that there is not a country on the globe more fertile in volcanic phenomena.

The mountains, which are all very lofty, are formed of lava and basalt; you cannot find there the slightest vestige of vegetable soil. In winter, the extreme cold splits these calcined mountains, and causes enormous fragments of them to fly off, which, in their fall, divide into a number of others, which roll precipitously into the roads and ways, like so many torrents, to overwhelm and obliterate the traces of them.

I was witness to several of these sorts of *avalanches*, which sometimes also take place in the fine season, but ever with a frightful noise, and a smell resembling that which arises from the calcination of bricks or lime-stone.

Not only the cold, but frequent earthquakes shake and over-throw the mountains of Iceland to their foundations; cleaving, disarranging, changing the direction of their constituent materials, which lose their consistence.

A number of mountains present extinguished craters; others are still ignivomous. In the interior of the island, some terrible eruptions took place in 1734, 1752, and 1755. The principal volcano, at present, is the mountain Krafte, which is ever emitting smoke and lava. Hekla, at the time of our stay there, was in a state of repose, but it has had new eruptions since.

Hot-springs and fountains are very numerous in the island; they excel all others known, in the abundance and degree of heat of their waters. The principal are, the springs of Gey-sen, situated at about two days walking journey from Hekla, and near Skalholt; they issue alternately from three succes-sive jetteaux of a considerable height. We saw one between Patrix Fiord and Lusbay, hot enough for the Icelanders to dress their victuals in.

The exterior geography of Iceland, that is to say, of the coasts, is as yet a desideratum for nearly the whole; the northern part is the least frequented, and the least known. The charts we had of them before the voyage of La Flore, had been copied from documents grounded on accounts of the Flemish and Dutch fishermen, and do not merit confidence. The chart published in 1767, in the French Neptune, is taken from M. Horrebow's; though better than the rest, with re-spect to the general configuration of the lands, it is full of errors as to the longitudes of places.

All the ancient Dutch charts place in the entrance, and about three leagues from the bay of Patrix Fiord, a group of ten islets, called Gouberman's Islands; there is not, however, the least trace of them. It is certain that the group must have formerly been in the situation, as the tradition of them is kept up in the country, and they have doubtless been over-whelmed, in consequence of some sub-marine convulsion. The same fate has probably carried away Pepy's Island, which is now no where to be found, but which stands in the ancient charts near the eastern coast of Iceland, in 64 degrees of latitude.

These extraordinary phenomena are of frequent occurrence, and they change, in some measure, the face of nature, and the general aspect of the coasts of the country. It does not appear, however, that they impede the progress of navigation; the shores are every where steep, the anchorage good, and the bottom is generally of volcanic gravel, or pebbles, and broken shells; and often the two substances are found united. There are on the coasts a number of deep bays, where ships may ride in perfect security, covered by the high lands that encircle them.

The general population of the island at present is about 40,000 souls; formerly it amounted to 60,000; but the scurvy, and especially the small-pox, which proved very fatal in 1707 and 1708, have greatly diminished the population, and are still very destructive. The governor-general, Van Tramp, who came to pay us a visit at Patrix Fiord, informed us that every year the number of deaths exceeded that of the births. In time, perhaps, the inhabitants of this country, who, besides, are addicted to insalubrious modes of living, will insensibly become extinct.

Iceland, subject to the crown of Denmark from the 13th century,* is rather an expensive charge than a profitable possession; the king only receives from it 140,000 francs per annum, and the whole of this scanty revenue is absorbed in the charges of the governor, of the bailiffs, and ecclesiastics, with the provisions and other expences of their household.

Notwithstanding its poverty, this country allured the cupidity of some Barbary corsairs, who, in 1626, landed here and carried off a number of the wretched inhabitants, whom they made slaves of. They were again visited in 1687, by other pirates, who practised the most horrid cruelties on the unfortunate natives, totally bereft of all means of defence.

These two examples are on record, yet the King of Denmark does not keep here any military force, nor have the Icelanders arms of any description; a gun, with powder and shot, is an object of curiosity, almost as much as with the inhabitants of the South-Sea Islands. We had pressing solicitations to indulge such curiosity, but it was only to expend in the chace; their peaceable character not suffering them to think of any other mode of application.

Of all other people, the Icelanders are, perhaps, those who have retained the primitive patriarchal manners in the greatest purity; they are good, loyal, hospitable, and unacquainted with any of those violent passions which, in other parts of the

---

* It was in the year 1261 that the Icelanders voluntarily submitted to Haquin, King of Norway.

world, lead men to act the part of butchers to each other. The Icelanders may, however, be characterised as indolent, and, in some respects, of an apathetic turn. An intimate union subsists among them; those of the same family seldom separate. The tenderness of parents for their offspring, the piety of these towards the authors of their being, are virtues of which we witnessed illustrious and affecting examples. No suspicion or distrust, one of the other, can be found here; theft and robbery are absolutely unknown; and, even during absence, the doors of their huts or cabins are always left open.

At the first glance, one would conceive the Icelanders to be the most wretched of men, the most destitute of the conveniences of life, and their condition to be the most frightful; but when we reflect on their unagitated character, on the few wants they feel, and the facility with which they can provide for them; if we consider, likewise, the sweet and intimate union that links them in the bonds of friendship, we must adopt another way of thinking, and even consider them as happier than the Europeans, whose enjoyments are mingled with so many perplexing circumstances, originating in ambition, in disappointments, in bodily infirmities, and the illusions and disquietudes of a thousand different passions.

The Icelander, satisfied with his lot, prefers his dreary country to all the charms of a more polished society in Europe. Such of them as have visited Copenhagen, in lieu of being smitten with the rural scenery of Denmark, were ever regretting their burnt mountains and eternal snows; and though numbers of them will turn out and volunteer, as seamen, on board Danish, or other vessels, they are sure in the end to return to their native isle, to mingle their ashes with those of their ancestors.

Although exiled, as it were, and having little communication with the rest of the world, the Icelanders are gifted with a quickness of intellect, and supplied with a measure of instruction which raises the lowest of them above the class of our villagers. In general, they speak Latin pretty well. In the eleventh century, science and literature were successfully cultivated here, while, at the same period, Europe was immersed in the depth of ignorance. Their MSS. composed at a period so remote, treat of astronomy, of physics, of natural history, of morals, and philosophy in general. Sir Joseph Banks, a celebrated naturalist, and worthy companion of Captain Cook, was in Iceland in 1772; he brought away 162 valuable MSS. which he presented to the British Museum.

The native language of the Icelanders is a very ancient dialect of the Celtic; it is not without its poetical effusions,

with songs or odes that turn on the heroic traditions of the
most distant times, and were recited by the bards, called
Scaldes. Their ancient mythology is exactly that of the
Scandinavians, from whom they are descended: thus their
traditions report the names of Odin and Frega; of Hella and
the goddesses Valkiries; the aerial combats of the Shades;
the delicious residence of Valhalla, or the palace of Odin,
wherein the spirits of departed heroes enjoy true felicity after
their decease.

I could only find in Iceland one single kind of antique
monuments; these are tumuli, or tombs of pebbles and small
stones heaped together; three of this description we recognised on the point of Vatneyre. All the voyagers who have
made mention of them, have represented these pyramidal
forms as raised expressly to point out the places of anchorage,
and to serve as beacons to vessels entering the bay; but the
director of the Danish factory assured me that they were ancient sepulchres, and he earnestly recommended to us to forbid
our men from despoiling or degrading them, as it would be a
serious affliction to the natives, who could not see us even approach them without symptoms of pain and uneasiness.

In France we have a great number of similar monuments,
which may be traced to the Celtic times; among others, is
one in the Morbihan, near the famous *men-hirs* of Carnak,
that stand in a row, and which rises nearly a hundred feet in
height.

The wood necessary for constructing their fishing-vessels
is brought from Denmark, for not a single tree is to be seen
on the island. The only fuel the inhabitants have is fish-
bones, with turfs of peat-moss, and a sort of *lignite*, or wood half
mineralised, and very bituminous, that is found in the mountains.

The Icelanders are extremely sober, but their unwhole-
some diet is productive of different diseases; it chiefly consists of raw fish, dried in the sun, and of sheep's-heads, preserved in a sort of vinegar, which they make with the juice
of sorrel. They eat also a sort of sea-weed (*fucus sacchari-
nus*), boiled in milk; and they make soup of the *lichen
Islandicus* reduced to powder. They are strangers to our
bread, and a fragment of worm-eaten biscuit was a treat to
them. Water and milk are their only beverage, and they ever
testified a great dislike for our wines and strong liquors.

Iceland may be considered as a very singular country, in
respect of its natural history, as yet but little known, and still
more so in a geological view, as teeming with observations
most curious and important. The mineralogist might here

collect a rich treasure of lavas, basalts, and pumices. In the vicinity of Patrix Fiord, we found beautiful crystals of feldspath, of analcime, of melonite, of amphigene, and zeolithe; these substances are commonly to be found in the cavities of the lavas.

I saw also, on the crater of an extinguished volcano, some octaedre crystals of native sulphur, involved in a whitish clayey substance; also the *obsidian* stone of the ancient mineralogists may frequently be met with.

There is no abundant variety of botanical plants in a climate so northerly, more particularly in the class of *Phanérogames*.

Here follows a list of the various species that I have observed:—

1	Fucus saccharinus.	27	Saxifraga aspera.
2	Fucus nodosus.	28	Saxifraga stellaris.
3	Fucus vesiculosus.	29	Salix lanata.
4	Fucus loreus.	30	Salix capraea.
5	Fucus carneus.	31	Carpinus betulus.
6	Fucus plumosus.	32	Dryas octopetala.
7	Ulva lactuca.	33	Pinguicula vulgaris.
8	Zostera marina.	34	Papaver alpinum.
9	Hypnum squarrosum.	35	Eriophoron vaginatum.
10	Minum fontanum.	36	Rhodiola rosea.
11	Lichen Islandicus.	37	Carex . . . .
12	Lichen chalybeïformis.	38	Barthia alpina.
13	Lichen spinosus.	39	Vaccinium vitis Idea.
14	Lichen muralis.	40	Silene rupestris.
15	Lichen rangiferus.	41	Silene arenaria.
16	Lichen paschalis.	42	Alsine media.
17	Lichen pixidatus.	43	Rumex scutellatus.
18	Juncus spicatus.	44	Allium . . . . .
19	Anthericum calycinum.	45	Cochlearia Groënlandica.
20	Draba muralis.	46	Sedum villosum.
21	Draba incana.	47	Thlaspi alliacea.
22	Saxifraga tridactylites.	48	Cerastium repens.
23	Saxifraga oppositifolia.	49	Geranium repens.
24	Erigeron uniflorum.	50	Ranunculus sulfureus.
25	Arabis thaliana.	51	Viola calcarata.
26	Polygonum viviparum.		

There is a greater variety in the productions of Zoology. The mamiferous animals of the island are—

1. The horse, which is small, but very numerous. It is of great use for travelling, walking with a sure step on the edge of precipices, and over the sharp fragments of basalt that lie in heaps in the paths.

2. The bull, or ox, is poor and lean, and the island is but scantily stocked with them.

3. The sheep are very numerous, of a good size, and commonly very fat. Most of the rams have four and even five horns.

4. The dog is about the size of our shepherd's dogs, which he pretty much resembles. The ears are straight, but gashed or broken at their extremities ; this is a character peculiar to the Iceland dogs.

5. The *Isatis*, or *Canis Lagopus* of Linnæus, is very common in Iceland. The natives call him the blue fox, from the slate-coloured tinge of his hair; he is very destructive to the flocks. Though a carnivorous animal, he will likewise eat grass, for I found a quantity of it in the stomach of a young one killed near Vatneyre. What was still more singular, we found in the viscera of this animal the opercules and other remnants of a shell-fish, common on the shore. I was not aware, till then, that mamiferous animals of this description would eat shell-fish, and particularly such whose shell is so hard; nor, I conceive, has the fact been hitherto noticed by naturalists.

6. The white bear is not a native of Iceland, but frequently arrives there on floating fragments of ice that are carried thither from the coasts of Greenland. On the appearance of these terrible animals, the inhabitants sound an alarm, and collect from every quarter to chace and destroy them before they have time to multiply.

7. The seal is very common. We saw more than once, round the bay of Leduc, another species of seal of the very largest dimensions, being eight or ten feet in length. The head, instead of terminating in a pointed muzzle, as in the preceding tribe, is large, wide, and much like that of a dog. The colour, taken altogether, of the animal, is that of grey ashes; unlike the rest of his genus, he is very shy and ferocious, and will let none approach him. I could only kill one of them.

8. The whale, designated by Linnæus as the *balæna mysticetus*, is less common here than at Spitzberg.

9. The gibber, or north caper, *balæna physalus*, is frequently met with on the coasts of Iceland.

Birds are in greater number and variety than the mammiferous animals; but the marine species are the most numerous. We saw none, however, that are not well known to ornithologists. Such as,

1 Aquila chrysaëtos.	10 Emberiza nivalis.
2 Aquila ossifraga.	11 Fringilla vulgaris.
3 Aquila Canadensis.	12 Charadrius auratus.
4 Falco haliætos.	13 Scolopax gallinago.
5 Falco communis.	14 Anas cygnus.
6 Falco candicans.	15 Anas fusca.
7 Strix scandiacca.	16 Anas anser.
8 Strix aluco.	17 Anas borealis.
9 Corvus corax.	18 Anas mollissima.

19 Alca arctica.
20 Alca alce.
21 Procellaria pelagica.
22 Procellaria glacialis.
23 Uria grylle.
24 Uria troile.

25 Colymbus immer.
26 Colymbus glacialis.
27 Larus rissa.
28 Larus eburneus.
29 Sterna hirundo.

We found no description of reptiles whatever on the island. Fish are in abundance, but with few varieties. The following are the several kinds:—

1 Pleuronectus hippoglossus.
2 Pleuronectus flesus.
3 Salmo salar.
4 Salmo trutta.

5 Gadus morhua.
6 Cyclopterus lumpus.
7 Anarrhicas lupus.
8 Squalus glaucus.

The seas which wash these coasts abound with the molusca and *radiaire*, but the short time of our residence in the island did not permit us to notice them all. The most common species are the *doris stellata* and *pilosa*, the *clios borealis* and *limacina*, the *asterias glacialis*, the *medusa capillata*, and the new kind which I have described under the name of *idya Islandica*.

The shells contain several new species of the tellina, the patella, and the buccinum; we also met with a very large species of *médiole*, the *pecten Islandicus*, the *buccinum nudatum*, and the lapillus; also some species of the *trochus*, of the meretrix mercatoria; as also of the common muscle and the sea-urchin, which are very good eating.

Insects are no strangers to the climate, notwithstanding its extreme rigour; but they are few in number, and mostly of the order of dipteres, and of the genera *culex, tipula, syrphus,* and *bibio* of Linnæus. I also met with a new species of the *curculio*, or weasle; and a very singular kind of nightbird.

There are several of the crustaceous kind, such as the *cancer*, or crab; the *maja*, the *crangon*, palæman, *gammarus*, &c.; and among the Zoophytes, some very beautiful species of corallines.

Such are part of the observations that I made during a stay of eighteen days, as well from my own researches as from the conversation with the physician to the governor, Van Tramp, a very intelligent character, who came at times to visit us, with all his suite, during our residence at Patrix Fiord. This gentleman, who had studied in the university of Upsal, had been a pupil of Linnæus.

A traveller that should make a longer residence in the island, and penetrate further into the interior, would find there a multitude of new facts, the narrative of which would be extremely interesting; this country, I repeat it, is almost entirely new to us with respect to its scientific reports and relations.

The Bay of Patrix Fiord is one of the most convenient points for the navigator; water, fish, and mutton, are in the greatest plenty; excellent game may be had, in several different sorts of sea-fowl; but wood is not to be procured at any price.

During our stay we set up some tents for our sick men, who very soon recovered, more especially from the use of the antiscorbutic vegetables that grow spontaneously in the island, and are frequently to be met with. The sea in this bay does not rise above eight feet in the highest tides. The variation of the needle was 33 deg. 45 min. to the N. W.

July 30, we hoisted sail, and leaving the Bay of Patrix Fiord, we bore away for the south, till we began again to distinguish Mount Jeugel ; soon after, bidding a final adieu to Iceland, we thought only of hastening our return to France.

Once more we passed over the point wherein the ancient charts placed the Isle of Bus, which we had before explored in vain; we were not more fortunate this time; but, as on the former occasion, we had to encounter a broken, rippling water, the usual indication of shoals and shallows.

On August the 18th, we were on the coast of Ireland ; we cruised there several days, at the entrance of the Bay of Donnegal ; we then steered for Cape Clear, which we doubled, to cruise on the *Soles ;* at last we entered the Channel ; and, on the 27th of September, cast anchor in the Road of the Isle of Brehut.

.

For EU product safety concerns, contact us at Calle de José Abascal, 56–1°, 28003 Madrid, Spain or eugpsr@cambridge.org.

www.ingramcontent.com/pod-product-compliance
Ingram Content Group UK Ltd.
Pitfield, Milton Keynes, MK11 3LW, UK
UKHW012337130625
459647UK00009B/350